THE

EVERYTHING KIDS'®

SCIENCE EXPERIMENTS BOOK

Boil ice, float water, measure gravity—
challenge the world around you!

Tom Robinson

Adams Media Corporation
Avon, Massachusetts

Note: All activities in this book should be performed with adult supervision. Likewise, common sense and care are essential to the conduct of any and all activities, whether described in this book or otherwise. Without limitation, no one should EVER look directly at the sun, as blindness could result. Parents or guardians should supervise children. Neither the author nor the publisher assumes any responsibility for any injuries or damages arising from any activities or outings.

An Everything® Series Book.
Everything® and everything.com® are registered trademarks of F+W Media, Inc.

Published by Adams Media, a division of F+W Media, Inc.
57 Littlefield Street, Avon, MA 02322
www.adamsmedia.com
ISBN 10: 1-58062-557-6
ISBN 13: 978-1-58062-557-9

Printed by RR Donnelley Harrisonburg, VA, USA

40 39 38 37 36 35 34 33 32

November 2014

Library of Congress Cataloging-in-Publication Data
Robinson, Tom, (Tom Mark).
   The everything kids' science experiments book / Tom Robinson.
      p. cm. — (Everything series)
   Includes index.
   ISBN 1-58062-557-6
   1. Science—Experiments—Juvenile literature. I. Title: Kids' science
experiments book. II. Title. III. Series.
Q164 .R625 2001
507.8—dc21   2001041276

This publication is designed to provide accurate and authoritative information with regard to the subject matter covered. It is sold with the understanding that the publisher is not engaged in rendering legal, accounting, or other professional advice. If legal advice or other expert assistance is required, the services of a competent professional person should be sought.

— From a *Declaration of Principles* jointly adopted
by a Committee of the American Bar Association
and a Committee of Publishers and Associations

Cover illustrations by Joseph Sherman.
Interior illustrations by Kurt Dolber. Additional contributions by Kathie Kelleher.
Puzzles by Beth Blair.
Series editor: Cheryl Kimball

Puzzle Power Software by Centron Software Technologies, Inc. was used to create puzzle grids.

This book is available at quantity discounts for bulk purchases.
For information, call 1-800-289-0963.

See the entire Everything® series at *everything.com*.

DEDICATION

For Matt and Megan

CONTENTS

ACKNOWLEDGMENTS

I would like to express my deep gratitude to Amy Biddle and her chemistry classes at Pinkerton Academy in Derry, New Hampshire, for reviewing my manuscript and experiments. I am also indebted to Vince Howard and the science department at Kentridge High School, Angie Lavine, Sara Dacus, and Jeff Renner at KING-TV for suggesting experiments, verifying the accuracy of the science concepts in the book, and reviewing the manuscript. Finally, I owe a debt of gratitude to my wife, Lisa, who allowed me to turn her kitchen into a science lab so my two young scientists and I could play and discover the joy of doing "spearmints" as a family.

INTRODUCTION

What does it take to be a great scientist? Think of the most famous scientists you know—Isaac Newton, Louis Pasteur, Albert Einstein, Thomas Edison, Pierre and Marie Curie, Stephen Hawking, and so on. What do all these people have in common? Well, for one thing, they're all very smart. In some cases they even taught themselves most of what they knew about their particular subject. In fact, Sir Isaac Newton had to invent a new branch of mathematics (calculus) just to solve the problems he was trying to do in physics. There is something else they all had in common that set them apart from the other smart people of their time—their ability to ask questions.

Just having a good brain isn't always enough. To be a great scientist, you need to be able to look at a problem that hundreds, maybe even thousands, of people have already looked at and been unable to solve, and ask the question in a new way. Then you take that question and come up with a new way to answer it. That is what made Newton and the others so famous. They coupled intelligence with a curiosity that said, "I want to know the answer to this." After coming up with the right questions, they discovered ways of answering those questions and ultimately became famous for their discoveries.

Could you be the next Thomas Edison and invent something the world has waited for, or the next Isaac Newton and answer a question no one has been able to answer? Absolutely! To do it requires something all kids have naturally and many grown-ups wish they still had—curiosity.

This book will help you to tap into that curiosity by introducing you to five major areas of science—Biology, Chemistry, Physics, the Earth and Sky, and the Human Body. You will be presented with several questions that will help you to begin thinking like a scientist. Perhaps you've asked some of these questions before; for example, why is the sky blue? Some of them will probably be new to you.

Since asking the right question is only the first step toward being a great scientist, this book will also guide you in completing the second step: the experiment. Following each question there will be an experiment that will help you discover for yourself some of the mystery and magic of science. There are three different types of experiments offered in this book— simple activities you can do quickly, larger and more complex experiments, and science fair projects.

Why did the young scientist bring art supplies to science class?

She wanted to draw some conclusions!

THE SCIENTIFIC METHOD

First, let's take a look at the starting point for all scientific experiments: the Scientific Method. It was made famous by an Italian man named Galileo in the sixteenth century. It is simple and will help you ask and answer many of the questions you have about science. There are five parts to the Scientific Method:

1. Observe some activity in the world around you.
2. Make up a possible explanation for that activity, called a hypothesis.
3. Use your hypothesis to make predictions about the activity.
4. Test those predictions.
5. Come to a conclusion about your hypothesis and its ability to predict the activity.

Scientists have used this method for hundreds of years to understand their world. Now it's your turn!

The fun of this book lies in the fact that you can start reading just about anywhere and follow the idea as far as you like. And if this book doesn't take the idea as far as you would like to go, use your imagination and keep exploring the idea. You are invited to join this exciting journey into the world of experimental science. Welcome aboard—let's begin the journey!

Quote Fall

Can you figure out where to put each of the scrambled letters? They all fit in spaces under their own column. When you correctly fill in the grid, you will have a quote from the brilliant scientist Albert Einstein. His theories and experiments led to an entirely new way of thinking about time, space, matter, energy, and gravity!

(All puzzle answers are located at the end of the book.)

	T	O		T	T		O					
	T	H		N	G	O	I	I		N	O	
Q	H	E	S	S	M	P	P	R	N	A	N	T
T	U	E	I	I	I	O	N	S	T	G		T

CHAPTER 1
BIOLOGY

Life. We all have it. The world around us is full of it, from the birds in the air to the fish in the sea and all the land animals in between. But how does life really work? If you can answer that question, you will gain insight into one of the most widely studied topics in the natural world.

TRY THIS WATER COLORS

Humans and other animals are very complex creatures. So let's first consider plants. Plants seem to be simple examples of the way life works. You plant them in the ground, water them, and let the sun shine on them. Pretty soon, they grow, they bloom, and then they die. But inside a plant, there are processes happening that we don't see—processes unlike anything else we encounter. Let's begin to understand these processes with what everyone knows is the most important resource a plant can get: water.

QUESTION

How does water get from the ground to the leaves of a plant?

MATERIALS

4 full glasses of water at room temperature
Red, blue, green, and yellow food coloring
3 white carnations from a florist
Sharp knife

PROCEDURE

1. Mix one color into each of your four glasses. The stronger the color of the water, the more effective the experiment will be.

2. Place your first carnation into the glass of your choice. You may need to trim the stem if it's too long.

3. Place your second carnation into another glass.

4. Take your final carnation and, with an adult's help, slice the stem lengthwise so that it looks like two smaller stems, both of which remain attached to the flower.

5. Place one half of the stem into your third glass of colored water and the other half into the fourth and final glass.

6. Place the flowers out of the sunlight and wait a day or so. Then look at each of the flowers.

WHAT'S HAPPENING

Through a process called **capillary action,** water travels up through the stems of plants until it reaches the outermost parts of the flowers. You saw this when the flower of each carnation turned the color of the water it was sitting in. Even more interesting is that the split stem produced a flower with *both* colors in it. You could easily repeat this experiment with other flowers and other colors to see if they behave in the same way. Celery stalks with the leaves on also work well in this experiment.

FOLLOW-UP

When you water the plants in your yard, should you water the leaves or the ground around the bottom of the plant?[1]

_____

_____

_____

_____

_____

_____

_____

_____

(The answers to all Follow-Up Questions are at the end of the book, starting on page 123. The number of the superscript marks the answer in the back.)

WORDS to KNOW

capillary action: the process that allows water and other nutrients to move up from the ground to all parts of a plant.

Why did the silly scientist keep his shirt on when he took a bath?

Because the label said "Wash and Wear."

Science Online

ZooNet is a good starting point for information about animals, zoos, and more. Visit *www.zoonet.org.*

TRY THIS
FALLING LEAVES

Some trees stay green the whole year round while others lose their leaves in the fall and winter and grow new leaves in the spring. If you've ever seen trees lose their leaves in the fall, you may have noticed that the leaves turn from green to yellow, red, or orange before eventually falling to the ground.

QUESTION

Where do the leaves get their colors?

MATERIALS

4–5 spinach leaves
1 drinking glass
Spoon
Nail polish remover—ask a parent for
    help in getting this
Coffee filter
Scissors
Tape
Pencil

PROCEDURE

1. Tear the leaves into small pieces.

2. Place the pieces into the bottom of the glass and mash them together with a spoon.

3. Add several teaspoons of nail polish remover to the leaf mush. Wait until the leaves settle at the bottom of the nail polish remover. If the remover does not cover all the leaves, add enough so that they are totally covered.

4. Cut a rectangle from the coffee filter. It should be slightly narrower than the glass.

5. Tape the rectangle to the pencil and, when the leaves are settled, place the pencil across the top of the glass so that the coffee filter rests in the nail polish remover without touching the leaves.

6. Let the glass sit for several hours.

Cool Quotes

Autumn is a second spring when every leaf is a flower.

—Albert Camus,
French novelist

WHAT'S HAPPENING

You should see many colors work their way up the coffee filter. The green you see comes from the chemical that makes leaves green—**chlorophyll**. But you should also see other colors, like red, yellow, and orange. These come from different chemicals that are also found in green leaves.

During the spring and summer, **photosynthesis** produces so much chlorophyll you can see only the green color in the leaves. But as the days get shorter, less chlorophyll is produced and the green fades away so that you can finally see the other colors. When the green is gone, the leaf is not far from falling to the ground.

FOLLOW-UP

When fall comes, watch the leaves change color. Can you tell what causes this to occur?[2]

_____

_____

_____

_____

_____

_____

_____

WORDS to KNOW

chlorophyll: the chemical in plants that makes their leaves green.

photosynthesis: the process by which plants turn sunlight and water into chlorophyll.

Fun Facts

Chlorophyll absorbs red and blue light and reflects green light back to your eyes.

What do you call a scientist who carries a dictionary in her jeans pocket?

A smarty pants!

KIDS' LAB LESSONS

QUESTIONS   Do seeds need light to grow? Do plants need light to grow?

EXPERIMENT OVERVIEW   You've already seen what happens to some trees when they don't get enough light—they lose their leaves. But plants and trees are different. In this experiment, you'll get to explore whether or not seeds and plants need light to grow by placing some seeds and plants in the dark while others stay in the light. You will decide whether or not light makes a difference in their growth pattern. This experiment will take a few days since most processes with plants occur very slowly, but the results should be obvious and a little surprising.

SCIENCE CONCEPT   Most gardeners believe that light and water are the basic needs of any plant. You'll test that theory by letting some seeds grow in a dark setting while others grow in a light setting. You'll then take two healthy plants and place one in a dark closet for a few days while the other sits in the sunshine. By doing this you will be using one of the most important pieces of the Scientific Method—testing one change at a time. It's important that you treat the seeds and plants exactly the same except for where they are placed. By doing so, you will know whether light makes a difference.

MATERIALS
2 paper towels
2 small dishes
Pinto beans (available at a grocery store)
Water
2 small, identical, healthy potted plants

PROCEDURE

1. Fold the paper towels so that each fits onto a dish.
2. Place the folded paper towel on a dish and place several beans on each paper towel.
3. Pour just enough water onto the paper towel so that it is damp. Pour out any excess water from the dish.
4. Place one dish of beans in a closet where it will stay dark for several days.
5. Water the potted plants until their soil is just damp and place one of the plants beside the beans in the same dark location.
6. Place the second dish of beans in a well-lit place alongside the second plant.
7. After two days have passed, slightly dampen the two dishes containing the beans and water the potted plants. Make sure that you give each the same amount of water so you keep the experiment fair.
8. After a total of four days have passed, take the beans and plant out of the closet and place each by its sunlit partner.

QUESTIONS FOR THE SCIENTIST

- Which sample of beans grew better—the one in the dark or the one in the light?

_____

- Which sample of potted plant grew better—the one in the dark or the one in the light? _____

- If you were going to plant seeds, where would you put them—in a light place or in a dark place? _____

- Think about the amount of light where seeds and plants normally grow. Does this experiment confirm that those locations are the best places for growing? _____

_____

- Do some seeds require different amounts of light? Experiment with different kinds of seeds and amounts of sunlight to see what factors most affect germination and growth. _____

Totally Tubular

Can you find your way through all the tiny tubes in this leaf from START to END?

END

START

TRY THIS HOLE-Y WALLS

Another amazing talent plants have is the ability to absorb water right through their skin. This process is called **osmosis,** and you can do an experiment that shows how it works.

QUESTION

Can liquid really pass through walls?

MATERIALS

2 wide glasses or measuring cups
Water
Tincture of iodine (available at a drugstore)
Cornstarch
A small, sealable plastic bag

PROCEDURE

1. Fill both glasses approximately three-quarters full of water.

2. In one glass, mix two teaspoons of iodine with the water.

3. In the other glass, mix one tablespoon of cornstarch with the water, and pour about half of it into the plastic bag.

4. Seal the plastic bag and place it into the iodine mixture. You may need to wash the bag with water to make sure there is no cornstarch on the outside when you place it in the iodine.

5. Allow the bag to sit in the iodine for an hour and observe the changes that occur during that time. Meanwhile, drop a few drops of iodine into the glass with cornstarch in it and observe what happens.

WHAT'S HAPPENING

The cornstarch mixture turns a dark color when iodine is present. This was proved when you dropped the iodine into the second glass. Iodine also turns color when in the presence of a starch. However, you didn't see the iodine mixture in the first glass ever turn color. Somehow, iodine has passed through the wall into the plastic bag, but the cornstarch was not able to pass into the iodine. Cornstarch molecules are large, compared to those of iodine. More important, iodine molecules are smaller than the holes in the plastic bag (yes, there *are* holes in those bags!), so they can pass through. However, the holes are too small to allow cornstarch molecules to pass so they are held inside the bag. Thus the iodine mixture remains its original color.

Fun Facts

Diffusion and osmosis are two ways cells can get the nutrients they need to grow and be healthy.

WORDS to KNOW

osmosis: a process in which liquids pass through the walls of cells.

Science Online

Learn about gardening from experts at Better Homes and Gardens. Visit *www.bhg.com/ gardening/*.

KIDS' LAB LESSONS

QUESTION   Can you blow up a balloon with a banana?

EXPERIMENT OVERVIEW   In this experiment, you will watch as a banana decomposes over time and inflates a balloon. The process is not something you can see, but the effects are unmistakable. As a follow-up, you can try other fruits to see if they produce the same results as they decompose.

SCIENCE CONCEPT   Eventually, plants die. A banana is the fruit produced by a banana tree, and anyone who has ever seen a banana ripen and turn brown before it could be eaten will know that as it ripens and dies, it undergoes dramatic changes. When a banana decomposes, **bacteria** flock to it. Bacteria are so small you can't see them. But not only are they there, they multiply and multiply by eating what's left of the banana. In this manner of processing food, they give off gas. Not a lot of gas, but with enough bacteria present, the gas will inflate the balloon. Your challenge, once you complete this experiment, is to try other fruits to see if they produce the same results.

MATERIALS
A very ripe banana
A bowl
A small-mouth plastic or glass bottle
A balloon

WORDS to KNOW

bacteria: tiny organisms that live in everything. Some can make you sick, but many of them help keep you healthy.

PROCEDURE

1. Peel the banana (make sure it is very ripe) and mash it in the bowl until the lumps are gone.
2. Carefully scoop the banana mush into the bottle. This might be a little tricky (and messy!), but with patience, it can be done. (You may also want to try using a plastic knife to scoop the banana mush into the bottle. This may be easier.)
3. Place the balloon over the mouth of the bottle.
4. Place the bottle in a warm, sunny spot and watch the bottle over the course of a few days.
5. Measure the distance around the balloon each day to track the progress of the banana's decay.

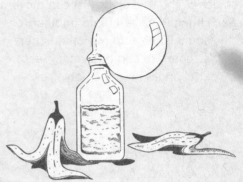

QUESTIONS FOR THE SCIENTIST

• What is causing the balloon to inflate? _____

• What is happening to the banana? _____

• How long did it take for the balloon to begin inflating? _____

FOLLOW-UP

Now that you have the procedure down, try mashing other ripe fruit (like apples, oranges, grapes, melons) and repeating the experiment. By comparing the growth rate of each fruit's balloon, you will be able to determine which fruit decays the fastest.

CLEAN-UP

Be sure to clean up this experiment near a sink or somewhere outside. The smell is likely to be unpleasant and strong. Carefully dispose of all your materials before starting over.

Scientific Transformation

Can you turn a banana into a balloon in four steps? Start with the word BANANA on line one. In each of the next steps you can move one letter, change one letter into another (or two of the same letters into two other letters that are the same), or add one letter. Keep track of your changes on the empty lines.

1. BANANA

2. _____

3. _____

4. _____

5. _____

Fun Facts
The largest worm ever found was 22 feet long.

ANIMALS

The animal kingdom includes more than 1 billion different sizes, shapes, and species. Some people spend their whole lives studying animals and barely even scratch the surface of all there is to learn. When you're a kid, though, some of the most interesting groups of creatures are found right in your backyard—the creepers, the crawlers, and the buzzers.

TRY THIS LIGHT FRIGHT

If you've ever been in your yard after a hard rain, or had the chance to dig up a large rock from your garden, chances are, you've run across a worm. Besides their being great for catching fish, most of us don't know a lot about worms. They may be a little odd to look at, and it may seem as though they don't serve much of a purpose, but worms are very important to the earth. They actually make soil better for growing.

QUESTION
Do worms prefer light or darkness?

MATERIALS

Shoe box	Earthworms, either from your
Scissors	yard or from a bait shop
Paper towels	Desk lamp

PROCEDURE

1. Cut off about one-third of the lid of the shoe box.

2. Thoroughly wet several pieces of paper towel and lay them on the bottom of the box.

3. Place the worms on the paper towels toward one end of the box. Try to space them evenly so they don't overlap one another. CAUTION: Make sure you handle the worms gently and with respect. A true scientist treats all creatures with care.

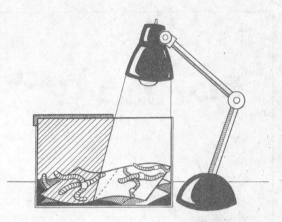

4. Place the lid on the box so the opening is on the same side as the worms.

5. Place the lamp above the box so that it sits about 1 to 2 feet higher than the top of the box.

6. Let the box sit for 15 to 30 minutes.

7. When you return, remove the lid and look at where the worms ended up.

WHAT'S HAPPENING

Worms tend to avoid light. That's why they like the dirt so much. When you shined the light into the box, most of them moved as far away from the light as they could get. In some cases, worms will even crawl under the paper towel to avoid the light. Worms can't see like we do, but they can sense light. When their **nervous system** senses the light, they immediately begin moving away from it.

FOLLOW-UP

With a hand-sized magnifying glass, look at the worm's circulatory system. After your experiment, return your worms to the garden where they will help your plants grow.

WORDS to KNOW

nervous system: the system our bodies use to tell us how things feel.

Science Online

Worm Digest has a large store of information about worms, composting, and gardening. Visit *www.wormdigest.org*.

KIDS' LAB LESSONS

If you've ever left fruit out on the counter a little too long, you've probably noticed the flies that seem to be attracted to it. Here is an interesting experiment to study about fruit flies.

QUESTION   What do flies like to eat?

EXPERIMENT OVERVIEW   You will be taking an overripe banana and leaving it to rot inside an open jar. Next to the jar with the banana will be a jar with nothing in it. In time, fruit flies will flock to the banana and help the decomposition process. Then, seemingly out of nowhere, small creatures called **maggots** will appear as well. Meanwhile, the empty jar will sit untouched. Once you have seen these results, you'll be ready to extend the experiment to try other possibilities.

SCIENCE CONCEPT   For many years, scientists believed that rotting fruit, like your banana, caused spontaneous generation. This means that life could spring up from nothing. Now we know that fruit flies eat the rotting fruit and use energy from the fruit to lay their eggs. Then we see the maggots. The fruit flies perform an important role. In a compost bin, leftover food is stored so that as it decomposes, it can be turned into nutrient-rich soil. The fruit flies help speed up that same process in your banana.

WORDS to KNOW

maggots: tiny wormlike creatures that grow into fruit flies.

MATERIALS

1 ripe banana

2 glass jars large enough to hold a banana

PROCEDURE

1. Peel the banana and place it into one of the jars. Leave the other jar empty.
2. Put the jars in a place they won't be disturbed for two weeks—preferably outdoors during warm weather.
3. Twice a day, observe the banana and keep a log of what you see. Include descriptions like color, consistency, smell, and the presence of flies or other living creatures.
4. Compare the contents of the empty jar to those of the jar with the banana.
5. After two weeks, look over your notes to mark the changes that occurred during that time.

QUESTIONS FOR THE SCIENTIST

• When did flies first appear? _____

• How long did it take for the banana to appear inedible? _____

• Where did the maggots come from? _____

• Can you think of any other creature that aids in the decomposing of discarded food? _____

FOLLOW-UP

Here are some variations on this experiment that you can try:

• Try putting a lid or a screen on the jar and see if you get the same results.
• Try another fruit, like an apple, orange, or a peach.
• Try placing the jars in different locations (light, dark, warm, cold, etc.).

TRY THIS
ANIMAL CAMOUFLAGE

If you know someone who has been trained in the military, you might have seen them in uniforms called fatigues. Sometimes they are called **camouflage** because these uniforms make it difficult for others to see the wearers when they are in hiding. But some animals, like the chameleon, do this naturally and serve as models for how to do it right.

QUESTION

How do animals blend into their surroundings?

MATERIALS

2 large sheets of construction paper in each of three different colors
Scissors
A partner

PROCEDURE

1. Cut one sheet of each color into 2-inch by 2-inch squares.

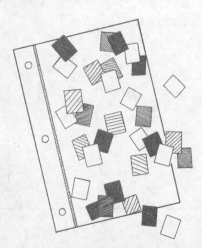

WORDS to KNOW

camouflage: how animals disguise themselves by blending into their surroundings.

2. Place all of the colored squares onto one of the large sheets while your partner closes his eyes.

3. When your partner opens his eyes, give him five seconds to grab as many colored squares as he can.

WHAT'S HAPPENING

Our eyes quickly notice sharp contrasts in color. You partner will usually pick out squares that are not the same color as the sheet they are lying on. When animals (and humans) use camouflage, they are taking advantage of the fact that when their colors match those around them (green frogs in grass, brown lizards on a tree branch) predators don't see any contrast, and the animals are somewhat hidden. If you placed a brown frog in the grass or a green lizard on a tree branch, that animal would stand out and would not be protected.

FOLLOW-UP

If you know someone who owns sunglasses called Blue Blockers, ask if you can try them on. When you do, what colors do you see most strongly? Do you know why this is?[3]

Eye Spy

Can you find the 10 creatures hiding in this picture?

KIDS' LAB LESSONS

QUESTION   Why are eggs shaped the way they are?

EXPERIMENT OVERVIEW   You will be exploring the shapes of eggs and the incredible strength they possess despite their fragile structure. By carefully preparing the eggs, you'll be able to place several books on top of four half-shells without cracking the shells. As a follow-up, you'll get to consider other versions of this test.

SCIENCE CONCEPT   Eggs are shaped the way they are for many reasons. A simple one is that the egg shape doesn't roll well. As a result, if a mother is sitting on her eggs and one gets away from her, it won't roll far before it comes to a stop. This allows the mother to quickly retrieve it. Try this before you begin the experiment. Gently roll an egg across the table or counter. Notice how its unique shape prevents it from rolling far like a ball would.

   Another reason for an egg's shape is that the dome shape gives it more strength than almost any other shape. Some people can place an egg in the palm of their hand and squeeze as hard as they can and not break the egg. The force of the hand is spread over the entire surface of the egg and nowhere is the force great enough to cause the egg to break. If you want to try this, you should either do it outside or in a large sink, for if you don't hold the egg just right, it will explode all over you!

MATERIALS
At least 4 raw eggs
Masking tape
Small scissors
Several books approximately the same size

PROCEDURE

1. Gently crack the eggs and break the shells as near to the middle (horizontally) as you can. If you don't get a good break, you'll need to try another egg.
2. Pour the raw eggs into a bowl and fry them up for your family.
3. Rinse and dry the empty half-shells.
4. Place one strip of tape around the open end of each shell, leaving the jagged edge exposed.
5. Use the scissors to trim off the jagged edges, taking care not to break the remaining shell.
6. You should now have four rounded egg bottoms and four pointed egg tops.
7. Select the rounded bottoms and place them in a rectangle on a table, approximately where the corners of your books will be.
8. Predict how many books your eggs will hold.
9. Gently add books until cracks first appear. This is the point when it becomes important that the egg supports are all about the same size. Note how many books caused the eggs to crack the first time.
10. Continue adding books until the eggs collapse.

QUESTIONS FOR THE SCIENTIST

- Did your eggs hold more or less books than you predicted? _____
- Why do you think the eggs can hold so much weight when they can be broken so easily on the side of a mixing bowl? _____
- What changes could you make to this experiment so that, still using eggshells, even more books could be supported? _____

FOLLOW-UP   Try using the pointed ends of the eggs and repeating the experiment. Which end of the eggshell held more weight?

Think about the magicians who lie on beds of nails. How does this experiment explain the "trick"? Think about the use of snowshoes in lands where a large amount of snow falls. Do these walking aids have anything to do with your egg experiment?[4]

SCIENCE FAIR PROJECT: BIOLOGY

GRAVITY

You probably haven't ever seen a plant growing down toward the ground with its leaves reaching for the dirt and its roots facing the sun. Why not? Plants seem to know which way is up, and they grow so that their roots grow down into the soil, while their leaves and flowers grow up toward the sun. As a budding scientist noticing this, your next step is to wonder exactly how it is that plants know to grow the way they do. It's the perfect reason to design an experiment!

QUESTION

How do plants know to grow upward?

EXPERIMENT OVERVIEW

In this experiment, you'll start by testing the reaction of a potted plant to being tipped on its side. Once you've seen how a mature plant behaves, you'll grow beans and test them to see if they know which way is up.

SCIENCE CONCEPT

Find a hill in your town with trees growing on it, the steeper the better. Look closely at the direction the trunks are growing and you'll see that they grow straight up despite the fact that the hill slopes below them. Plants have a knack for sensing gravity and growing their roots down while the stems and leaves grow vertically upward. This is because of a chemical they have called auxin. Auxin makes plants grow longer and when gravity acts, the auxin tends to fall to the low side of a plant and its leaves. This makes the lower sides of the stem and leaves grow slightly longer, which turns the plant upward. Roots act differently, as they are a different part of the plant. On the root, the auxin causes slower growth. So, when auxin gathers on the lower side of the root, the upper side grows a little longer and the root turns downward. You'll get to observe both cases in this experiment.

MATERIALS

3 small, mature potted plants
Sunny location
Drinking glass
Water

Several pinto beans
Paper towel
Aluminum foil
Camera

PROCEDURE

MATURE PLANTS

1. Place all three potted plants in a sunny location, but tip one on its side toward the sun, tip another on its side away from the sun, and leave the third upright.

2. Water each plant as you would normally (you can turn them right-side-up to water them) and record their growth. This part of the experiment may take longer with some plants, so be patient. However, it shouldn't take too long for the tipped plants to try to right themselves.

SEEDS

1. Soak the beans in the glass filled with water overnight before starting.

2. Pour out the water and place the beans to one side of a paper towel, folded in half.

3. Carefully, roll the beans up in the paper towel and wet it just so it's moist, but not dripping.

4. Fold a piece of aluminum foil around the paper towel so that the entire towel is covered and sealed.

5. Place the aluminum foil containing the beans into the glass with one end up and let the beans sit for one week.

6. After a week has passed, open the foil and carefully unroll the paper towel. Do not touch the beans as you will be using them again. You will be reusing both the foil and paper towel as well, so take care not to rip either.

7. Record the direction of growth of both the stem parts of the beans and the roots. They should be just beginning to grow and show that they have found "up" despite their orientation when you put them in the glass.

8. Take a picture of the beans to document their growth.

9. Moisten the beans as before, repack them in the paper towel and aluminum foil, and return them to the glass. But this time point the end that was originally up toward the bottom (turn the foil upside down).

10. After another week passes, open the foil and record the new growth. You should notice that after the original direction of growth, the beans adjusted to being placed upside down and continued their growth in the "right" direction. Take another picture for documentation.

QUESTIONS FOR THE SCIENTIST

- What did you observe about the growth of the potted plants?

- Was there a difference between the growth of the plant tipped toward the sun and the plant tipped away from the sun?

- How do you know that it was gravity and not the sun or another factor that made the plants grow the way they did?

- Did the beans grow in the direction you expected during the first week?

- After the second week, did the direction of the stems and roots change?

- Why do you think this change occurred?

- Can you tell that the beans started in one direction and then changed? How can you tell?

CONCLUSION

From the time they are just seeds, plants have the ability to know which way is up and immediately begin growing in that direction. Mature plants already have their root system in place, but will continually adjust the direction of stem and leaf growth in order to find up. Some plants that grow very tall will actually wind their way through and around obstacles in order to find their way up.

As a follow-up, you can plant your beans in soil by placing them on their sides and watch them adjust once more to the direction of gravity. Soon enough, the stems will pop through the soil and the roots will find their way to the bottom.

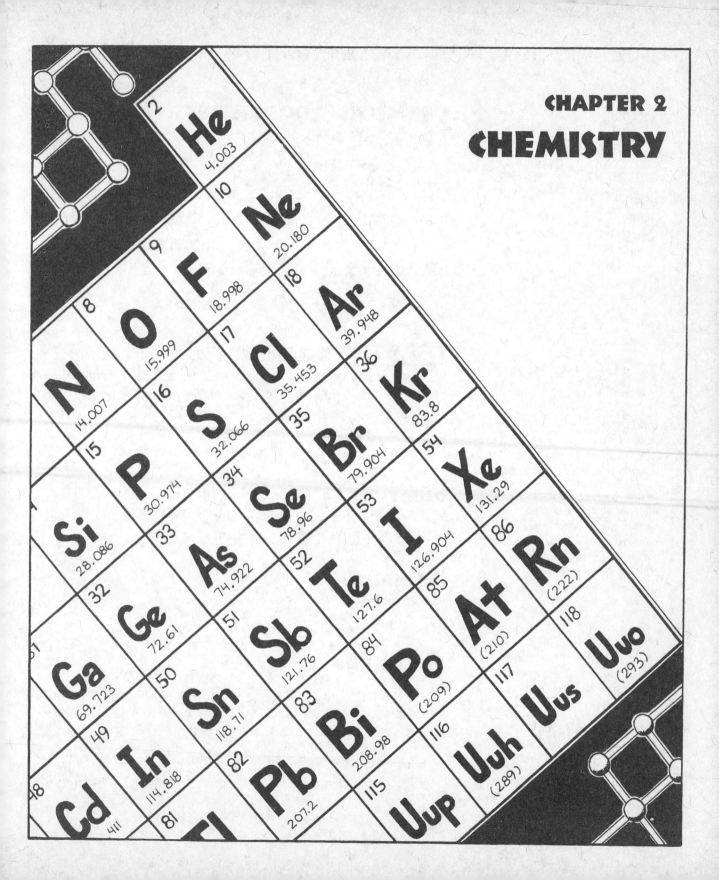

Fun Facts

When lakes freeze in the winter, they freeze from the top down. So as the top freezes, the water below is actually protected from the cold by the ice. This is how fish can survive.

WORDS to KNOW

solid: a state in which a material is hard and usually very dense. A solid will maintain its shape even outside a container.

liquid: a state in which a material is a fluid and is less dense than a solid, yet more dense than a gas. A liquid will assume the shape of its container, but won't expand in the container to do so.

gas: a high-energy state in which a material is a collection of molecules moving in random motion generally at high speeds. A gas will assume the shape of its container, but it will expand or compress in order to do so.

Second Law of Thermo-dynamics: heat always flows from a hotter object to a colder object.

CHEMICAL PROPERTIES

All materials you can see and many you can't are grouped by certain characteristics. Examples of these characteristics include density, pressure, temperature, volume, phase, and atomic makeup. In this chapter we'll look at questions relating to all of these, but we'll focus on phase, density, and pressure.

TRY THIS BOILING ICE

Most materials with mass usually exist in three different phases: **solid**, **liquid**, or **gas**. Each of these phases has its own set of unique properties, and those properties describe the material in very special ways. Take water, for example. Do you know what it looks like in its solid, liquid, and gas forms?

QUESTION

Why does a pot of boiling water stop boiling when an ice cube is put in it?

MATERIALS

Pot of water   Several ice cubes
Stove

PROCEDURE

1. Set the pot of water on the stove and turn the burner on high until the water boils. You might need to ask for permission or some assistance for this step.

2. Once the water has come to a steady boil, place several ice cubes into the pot, keeping the water boiling. Observe what happens.

WHAT'S HAPPENING

The boiling should have stopped immediately. Why is this? It's because of the **Second Law of Thermodynamics.** According to this law, the heat coming from the burner will always flow to the coldest object in the pot—in this case, the ice. So the heat from the burner stops making the hot water boil and starts making the solid water melt.

FOLLOW-UP

When the ice finally melts, will the water start boiling right away?[1] Once the water boils again, notice the steam that rises from the pot. Where does it come from? It's just the same water in another state, a gas, and it's called water vapor. We see it when we take a shower in a cold room, and whenever we see clouds or fog in the sky.

_____

_____

_____

_____

_____

Fun Facts

It takes nearly seven times more energy to melt 1 kilogram of ice than it does to boil 1 kilogram of water!

TRY THIS
FLOATING GRAPE

One of the many ways you can describe a material is by its density. Density is nothing more than the measure of how solid something is. For example, water is less solid than a chunk of concrete, and its density is less than that of concrete. Scientists use a formula involving mass (how much of the material there is) and volume (how much space the material takes up) to figure out an object's density. The less dense it is, the less tightly packed the particles are, and the more space it tends to take up.

Density is what makes balloons float up in the air, ice cubes float in your drink, and rocks sink to the bottom of a lake. But it can also be tricky! Here's a fun trick that is guaranteed to amaze your friends.

QUESTION

Can you make a grape float in the middle of a glass of water?

Cool Quotes

The whole of science is nothing more than a refinement of everyday thinking.

—Albert Einstein

MATERIALS

4 drinking glasses
Masking tape
Marker
1 larger glass or measuring cup
Water and sugar
Grapes
A spoon

PROCEDURE

NOTE: Before you do this for an audience, you should practice this by yourself. When you are ready to perform, you should have the glasses already prepared.

1. Using the masking tape and marker, label each glass as "#1," "#2," "#3," and "#4."

2. Fill the measuring cup with water and stir in enough sugar so that a grape will float at the surface of the water. If some sugar remains undissolved, allow it to fall to the bottom of the cup.

3. Fill Glass #1 full of water.

4. Place one grape into Glass #1 and observe what happens to it.

5. Fill Glass #2 with the sugar water solution you already prepared.

6. Place one grape into the sugar water solution. You should see it float at the surface.

7. Now fill Glass #3 half-full of the sugar water solution.

than the solution. If you prepare the solution far enough in advance, it will be almost impossible to detect the separation between the plain water and the sugar water.

FOLLOW-UP

With the final glass (#4), experiment to see if you can come up with a new sugar water solution that, when fully mixed, will cause the grape to float in the middle just like in Glass #3.

8. Slowly and carefully fill the rest of Glass #3 with plain water, taking care NOT to mix the heavier sugar water below it. You might want to place a spoon just inside the glass and pour the water so it falls onto the spoon before it hits the sugar water. This step may take a few tries to master, but when you are done, you should find that you can't tell the difference between the two liquids in Glass #3.

9. Place a grape gently into Glass #3 and observe what it does.

WHAT'S HAPPENING

The grape is denser than the water, so it sinks immediately to the bottom of the glass. The sugar water solution contains more matter in the same glass, so it is denser than the plain water. It is also denser than the grape, so the grape floats on top. The third glass is your "trick" glass. You know what is in it, but your unsuspecting audience does not. The grape sinks through the water, as it is denser than the water, but it floats on the surface of the sugar water solution since it is less dense

Fun Facts

The density of the sun is 1.41 times that of water. Here are the densities of the sun and all the planets in our Solar System as multiples of the density of water.

Sun:	1.41
Mercury:	5.43
Venus:	5.42
Earth:	5.52
Mars:	3.93
Jupiter:	1.33
Saturn:	0.69
Uranus:	1.32
Neptune:	1.64
Pluto:	2.06

KIDS' LAB LESSONS

QUESTION   Can you make a liquid float?

EXPERIMENT OVERVIEW   You will be pouring liquids with different densities into the same container and producing a layered solution. Using colors, you will show how additional liquids poured into your solution find their way to the "right" layer. You will also "clean" some of the colored water and be invited to consider other possible color patterns.

SCIENCE CONCEPT   Ice cubes float in water because ice is less dense than water. In the same way, an oil spill tends to ride on the surface of the water because oil is also less dense than water. However, solid objects, or even thicker liquids, will sink in water because they are denser than the water. To compare the densities of two or more materials, you can set up a liquid test container with layers of liquids, each with different density. By noticing how the materials separate from one another, scientists can identify unknown materials. This makes it easier to clean up pollution in lakes and streams.

MATERIALS
Red and blue food coloring
Measuring cup
1 cup corn syrup
Clear glass bottle—empty 24–32-ounce glass bottles
    work well
1 cup vegetable oil
½ cup water
½ cup liquid bleach (Be very careful with bleach. Always
    ask for an adult's help before using it.)

Fun Facts

The air we breathe is composed of several gases, but the two major ones are nitrogen and oxygen. The percentages are:

nitrogen (78%)
oxygen (21%)
other gases (1%)

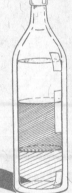

Fun Facts

Did you know both cement and steel can float? Due to the Archimedes Principle, which says that objects are supported by a force equal to the weight of the water they displace, even heavy ships, if they are designed right, can float!

PROCEDURE

1. Mix red food coloring into a measuring cup filled with the corn syrup. Pour the syrup into the bottle.
2. Pour the oil into the bottle on top of the corn syrup. Do these liquids mix?
3. Mix blue food coloring into a measuring cup filled with the water. Pour the water into the bottle on top of the oil. Give it several minutes to settle. Where does the water go when you pour it into the bottle? Can you explain why it does this?
4. At this point, you should have three distinct layers in your bottle. The bottom layer will be red; the middle, a thinner layer of blue; and the top layer will be clear.
5. Now pour the bleach into the mixture and observe what happens to the blue water. Again, allow several minutes for the mixture to settle.

QUESTIONS FOR THE SCIENTIST

- What happened to the blue water? _____
- Can you describe where the bleach ended up? _____
- Why didn't the bleach mix with the syrup? _____

CONCLUSION   The first three liquids all have different densities and exist in layers in the bottle. When you added the bleach, it sank through the oil, because it is denser than oil. It is not as dense as corn syrup, so it did not sink through the bottom layer. This put it at the same layer as the blue water and it happens to mix easily with water. So the bleach and water were mixed and the bleach turned the blue water clear again!

FOLLOW-UP   It would be fun to make a mixture that has red, white, and blue bands, in that order. This would mean dyeing the oil (the top layer) either red or blue. Why isn't this possible in the setup you are using? _____

_____

TRY THIS

FLOATING WATER

Air is all around us. We breathe it, we use it to inflate the tires on our car, and we feel it when the wind blows. One of the surprising aspects of air is that we can't see it, we can't taste it, and only in certain cases can we feel, hear, or smell it. Yet it is a critical piece of our lives.

When air is in a container, it exerts pressure on its surroundings. This pressure is what creates wind and weather, it's what makes airplanes fly, it's what makes curve balls curve, and it's what keeps your car tires inflated and able to roll on the road. Simply put, air pressure is a part of everything we do.

Here's an easy magic trick to do that isn't really magic. Once you understand how air pressure works, you can amaze your friends once with the demonstration and then again when you explain how it works!

QUESTION

Can you make water float in the air?

MATERIALS

A small cup of water, clear plastic works best

A sink, bathtub, or tray to catch any water that falls while you practice this demonstration

A note card or other small piece of paper (the card must be large enough to fully cover the top of the cup)

PROCEDURE

1. Fill the cup about three-quarters full of water. The amount of water isn't that important, although you may find it more difficult to do this if the cup is full.

2. While the cup is held over the sink, slowly turn it over and observe how the water pours out of the cup.

3. Now refill the cup with water and place the card on top of the cup, making sure that it covers the entire top.

4. Press down gently but firmly on the card as you slowly rotate the cup upside down.

5. Keep your hand on the card for a few moments, then remove your hand. The card should stay in place and the water will appear to float inside the cup with nothing holding it up.

Cool Quotes

Imagination is more important than knowledge. Knowledge is limited. Imagination encircles the world.

—Albert Einstein

Egg-sactly!

Can you fill in the blanks to finish the following common sayings about eggs? Choose words from the Word List found in the bottom of the bottle.

WHAT'S HAPPENING

When you tipped the cup over the first time, the water ran out because gravity pulled it down toward the sink. The only way to prevent this from happening is to find some force that counteracts gravity. Enter air pressure.

When you add the card, you see the effects of air pressure. The air below the cup actually pushes up on the card, just like it pushes on everything around you. In this case, the upward force of air pressure is enough to cancel out the effect of gravity on the water and keep the water "floating" inside the cup.

Depending on the strength of the card you use, you may notice that eventually some water begins to leak out. As this happens, the seal begins to break and the card is no longer able to prevent gravity from winning the battle. Soon all the water will spill out.

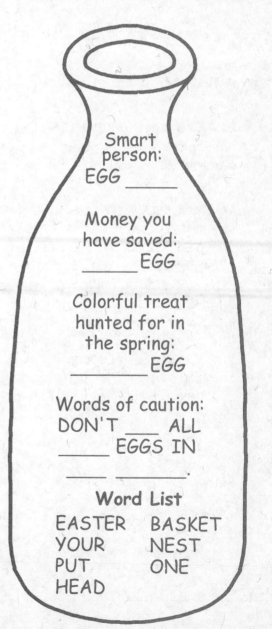

Smart person:
EGG _____

Money you have saved:
_____ EGG

Colorful treat hunted for in the spring:
_____ EGG

Words of caution:
DON'T ____ ALL _____ EGGS IN ____ _____.

Word List

EASTER   BASKET
YOUR   NEST
PUT   ONE
HEAD

KIDS' LAB LESSONS

QUESTION   Can you push an egg into a bottle without touching it?

EXPERIMENT OVERVIEW   Air has the ability to make objects move into and out of places where they otherwise would not fit. In this experiment, you will force a hard-boiled egg into a bottle without touching the egg.

SCIENCE CONCEPT   Air has an interesting behavior. It always flows from high pressure to low pressure. That is why when you get a hole in a tire on your bicycle the air leaks out. In this experiment, you'll be placing a hard-boiled egg between high pressure (the outside air) and low pressure (the air inside the bottle). Air wants so badly to get inside the bottle, it will push away anything in its way (the egg)! You'll use this principle to get the egg in.

To make it work, you will have to lower the pressure inside the bottle so much that the outside air forces the egg into the bottle. You will do this by placing lit matches inside the bottle. The matches will burn until the oxygen inside the bottle has been consumed. At this point, there is less air (since some of it was consumed by the fire) inside the bottle than there previously was, which results in decreased air pressure. As the outer air pushes into the bottle, the egg slides in.

MATERIALS
Wide-mouth bottle (20–32-ounce juice bottles will work but make sure that the egg
   is just barely too big. If the opening is too small, the egg will probably get stuck.)
1 hard-boiled egg with the shell removed
3 matches
A very small piece of paper (1" × 1")

PROCEDURE

Insertion

1. Place the hard-boiled egg on the mouth of the bottle. It should sit comfortably without falling off. You may try to push the egg into the bottle to verify that it does not easily fit.
2. Remove the egg and place three lit matches into the bottle with the paper. Use matches only with adult supervision!
3. Quickly replace the egg on the mouth of the bottle, effectively sealing the top of the bottle.
4. Watch as the matches go out and the egg is pulled down into the bottle.

Removal

1. Turn the bottle upside down so the egg falls into the opening without coming out. Blow into the opening. (It is recommended to have an adult do this part.)
2. As the pressure inside the bottle increases, the egg should be pushed out of the bottle into your mouth.

QUESTIONS FOR THE SCIENTIST

- Why did the egg get pushed into the bottle? _____

  _____

- What did the burning matches have to do with this experiment? _____

  _____

- What are some other examples of air flowing from high pressure to low pressure?

  _____

WORDS to KNOW

acid: materials that taste sour, like lemon. If strong enough, these can burn your skin.

base: materials that taste bitter, like ground coffee. If strong enough (for example, ammonia or bleach), these can also be dangerous.

Fun Facts

pH is what scientists use to measure the acidity of a substance. A pH value of 7.0 is called neutral, while a value higher than 7.0 indicates a base. pH values lower than 7.0 indicate acids. Here are some sample pH values for common foods:

Food	pH
Lemons	2.3
Strawberries	3.2
Tomatoes (whole)	4.6
Potatoes	6.1
Sweet corn	7.3
White eggs	8.0

CHEMICAL REACTIONS

Have you ever taken a bite of a lemon and had your mouth pucker up because it was so sour? Have you ever wondered why some foods taste the way they do? One reason is because of things called **acids** and **bases.** Lemons and other citrus fruits are filled with citric and ascorbic acids (vitamin C), which provide a wide range of health benefits. But they also make them taste sour. On the other hand, some foods we eat are called bases. They are on the other end of the acid scale and taste bitter. Bases include items such as baking soda (to make baked goods rise), antacid tablets (to help against indigestion and heartburn), and some soaps.

TRY THIS
RED CABBAGE INDICATOR

There are plenty of fancy ways to test to see if something is an acid or a base, but you can also do it simply in the comfort of your own home.

QUESTION

How can you figure out if something is an acid or a base?

MATERIALS

Cabbage **indicator**—the liquid from a jar of pickled red cabbage, available at the grocery store
Eyedropper

1 small plate for each of the materials you wish to test. Below
   are some samples:
   Lemon juice
   Orange juice
   Baking soda
   Vinegar
   Antacid tablet
   Tea bag—mix with water to make tea
   Ground coffee

PROCEDURE

1. Pour some of the indicator into several small plates.

2. Drop a small amount of each test item onto a plate and
   watch what happens to the indicator.

Cool Quotes

The most exciting phrase
to hear in science, the
one that heralds new
discoveries, is not
"Eureka!" (I found it),
but "That's funny...."

—Isaac Asimov,
author and biochemist

WHAT'S HAPPENING

With some of the test samples, the indicator will turn a pink
color. That is your clue that you've tested an acid. Other samples should have turned the indicator greenish blue. Those are
the bases. Now that you know what to look for, can you find
other acids and bases in your kitchen?

CAUTION: Some acids are very dangerous to humans. Be
careful not to get any of the samples on your skin, and never
try to eat or drink things that you are experimenting with.

TRY THIS
RAW EGG PEELER

Now that you know how to find acids, you are ready to see what an acid can do to a common kitchen item.

QUESTION

How can you peel a raw egg?

MATERIALS

Raw egg   Vinegar   Small glass

PROCEDURE

1. Place the egg into the glass.

2. Pour enough vinegar into the glass to cover the entire egg.

3. Let it sit for a few days.

4. You should return to find that the eggshell has disappeared and your raw egg has become see-through. You may need to rub the surface to remove the last parts of the shell.

WHAT'S HAPPENING

The acid in vinegar slowly ate away at the eggshell until none of it remained. When you returned to find the see-through egg, you were really seeing the thin membrane that holds the egg inside the shell. You may have noticed quite a bit of bubbling during the "peeling" process. Eggshells are made of calcium carbonate, which reacts with vinegar (an acid) and makes calcium acetate, carbon dioxide (the bubbles you see), and water.

Amazing Bubbles

Can you find your way from START to END without bursting any of the bubbles?

TRY THIS
FOAMING AT THE MOUTH

You put something in your mouth every day that has the ability to produce bubbles in a similar fashion to the previous experiment. However, this doesn't involve any acids, just toothpaste and a can of soda.

QUESTION

How can I make myself foam at the mouth?

MATERIALS

Baking soda toothpaste   **Carbonated soda** or water
Toothbrush   Sink

PROCEDURE

1. Brush your teeth with the toothpaste as you normally would.

2. Instead of spitting when you are done, open your mouth and take a sip of the carbonated soda or water. You should feel fizzing in your mouth.

3. Open your mouth and let the foam come rolling out!

CAUTION: This should be performed only under adult supervision. Also, make sure you have a place for the foam to flow into. Never try to swallow it or keep it in your mouth. You could get very sick from swallowing too much of this mixture.

WHAT'S HAPPENING

The ingredients of baking soda toothpaste are designed to make some bubbles, as you've probably noticed during your normal brushing routine. Adding the carbonated beverage, which has carbon dioxide gas, produces a reaction that will keep the bubbles coming and coming.

carbonated soda: a soft drink that has carbon dioxide gas in it, making it fizzy.

Fun Facts

New dental cleaning techniques involve using baking soda as an abrasive in place of scraping.

Baking soda toothpaste is an effective way of removing crayon marks from walls.

KIDS' LAB LESSONS

QUESTION   What makes things fizzy?

EXPERIMENT OVERVIEW   In this experiment, you will produce different combinations of mixtures that react to form fizzy **solutions.** You'll start with a baking soda/vinegar mixture, and then move on to make your own safe-to-drink, though not particularly tasty, lemon soda.

SCIENCE CONCEPT   Certain materials, when brought into contact with other materials, react in a way that forms bubbles. Acids and bases often combine to form carbon dioxide, which, as a gas, is what makes carbonated soda fizzy. You'll be experimenting with several common ingredients to determine which react in this way.

MATERIALS

Part I
½ cup vinegar
20-ounce glass bottle
2 tablespoons baking soda
¼ cup water

Part II
Food coloring
A pitcher of water
3 teaspoons baking soda
2 tablespoons sugar
2 tablespoons lemon juice

Part III
Large glass filled with water
Small (¼ pound at the largest) piece of dry ice (available at many grocery stores or fish markets—you may need an adult to buy and handle it for you)

WORDS to KNOW

solution: a mixture of two or more liquids.

PROCEDURE

Part I

1. Pour vinegar into the bottle.
2. Dissolve baking soda in water and pour the mixture into the bottle.
3. Watch what happens.

Part II

1. With the food coloring, color the water in your pitcher any color you like. This is just for looks, but you will be able to drink your concoction when you are done, so pick a color you would like to drink.
2. Stir in baking soda and sugar. Mix until they dissolve.
3. Add lemon juice and watch your drink become carbonated!

Part III

1. Place the dry ice in the water and watch what happens. CAUTION: Dry ice is very cold and should be handled only with gloves with close adult supervision.

QUESTIONS FOR THE SCIENTIST

- What kinds of materials reacted to make bubbles? _____

- How did your soda taste? Can you think of any ingredients you could add to improve the taste? _____

- Would your lemon drink work with any other fruit's juice? Which fruits do you think would work? _____

- Could you use dry ice to make a carbonated soft drink? _____

What size T-shirt do you buy for a 200-pound egg?

Eggs-tra Large!

Science Online

For a fun look at how money is made and how much money is made, check out the U.S. Mint's Web site at *www.usmint.gov*.

TRY THIS CLEANING PENNIES

Some chemical reactions can take dirty objects and make them clean by removing the dirt. Detergents do this with the dirt on your clothes and your dishes, and the soap you use in the bath or shower does the same for your body. But what about metals? They are harder to clean.

QUESTION

How do you clean a penny?

MATERIALS

Vinegar
Glass jar
Dirty pennies
1 teaspoon salt

PROCEDURE

1. Pour vinegar into the jar until it is about half full.

2. Stir in salt until it dissolves.

3. Drop several dirty pennies into the vinegar.

4. After a few minutes, take out half of the pennies and lay them on a paper towel to dry.

5. Remove the other pennies and rinse them with water before letting them dry.

6. Note the differences between the two groups of pennies after they have been out of the vinegar/salt solution for a while.

WHAT'S HAPPENING

The vinegar/salt solution is able to loosen the residue on the pennies, which is called copper oxide. With this residue removed, the pennies are shiny once more. When you rinse them off, the cleaning stops and they remain shiny. The unrinsed pennies still have some of the solution on them, and when oxygen in the air hits them, a new reaction occurs, turning the pennies a bluish-green color.

FOLLOW-UP

Try this same experiment with nickels, dimes, and quarters. Do you get the same results?[2]

_____

_____

_____

_____

_____

_____

_____

_____

Acid Bath

Oops! This young scientist tried to clean his friends' copper ID bracelets. But the acid was too strong and it removed part of each letter! Question: Can you add the missing lines to complete the letters and see to whom each bracelet belongs?

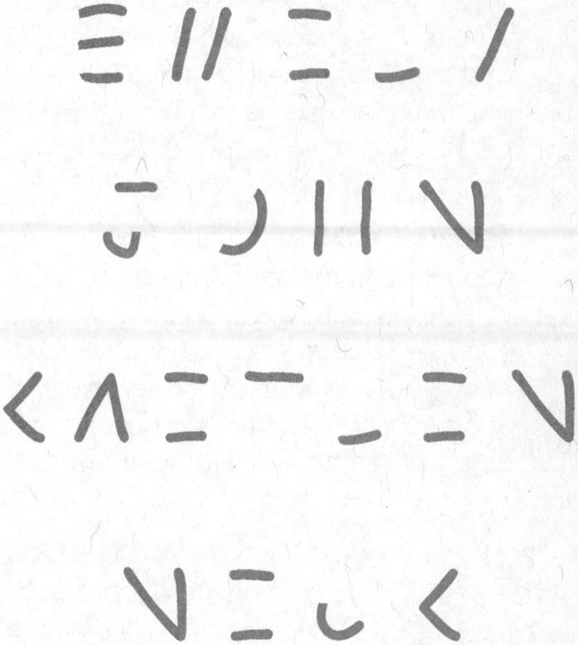

$E=mc^2$

KIDS' LAB LESSONS

QUESTION   How are metal things made shiny?

EXPERIMENT OVERVIEW   Electroplating is the process of taking a metal and using it to coat something else. It is a complex process involving electricity and is difficult to perform in a home laboratory. This experiment is not electroplating in the true sense, but it does produce a transfer of copper from the pennies to the nails.

SCIENCE CONCEPT   It's possible to remove atoms of a material (like copper) and have them float around in a liquid without you seeing them. To retrieve them, you simply need to make them want to attach to the metal you want to coat. In this case, the vinegar/salt solution removes copper oxide atoms (the "dirt" on the pennies), and when they dissolve, they form copper atoms that want to attach to another metal. The nails attract the copper atoms floating in the water, and the atoms stick to them, coating them with copper.

WORDS to KNOW

electroplating: a process that uses one metal to coat another metal.

MATERIALS
Vinegar/salt solution prepared as described in the
    "Cleaning Pennies" activity on page 40
Two clean nails or metal paper clips
Dirty pennies

PROCEDURE

1. Prepare a solution of vinegar and salt as described in the previous activity.
2. Soak the dirty pennies in the vinegar/salt solution until they are clean.
3. Remove the pennies and set them aside.
4. Place your nails into the remaining solution and let them sit for a few hours.
5. When you are ready to remove the nails, remove them carefully and look closely to see if they have changed color. If they have not done so noticeably, return them to the solution. If you want to speed up the process, place more dirty pennies in the solution along with your nails.

QUESTIONS FOR THE SCIENTIST

• What is the coating on the nails? _____

• Why can't you see that coating in the solution before you place the nails in it?

_____

CONCLUSION

You are observing a pretty amazing process. The acid solution not only removes the dirt (which is a combination of copper and oxygen called copper oxide), but in doing so, leaves copper atoms floating in the solution. These atoms are so small you can't see them, but they will float in the acid solution until they find a negatively charged metal to stick to. When you place the nails in the acid, some of their atoms are also removed and they are left with a negative charge. The copper atoms are attracted to the nails and stick to them, giving them a slight copper tint.

SCIENCE FAIR PROJECT: CHEMISTRY

BUILD A HOME BAROMETER

When you watch the evening news, the weather reporters often refer to the baro-metric pressure as an indicator of both current conditions and the predicted weather. In particular, they will tell you if the pressure is rising or falling. Generally, falling pressure, or the presence of a low pressure system, indicates bad weather, and rising pressure, or the presence of a high pressure system, indicates improving weather. When air warms up, pressure tends to increase, while cooling air is usually accompanied by lower pressure. You will also find this if you climb a mountain. At the higher elevations, the air is thinner, which means the pressure is lower, and the air is also usually cooler.

It's not hard to build your own barometer that will allow you to predict the weather from the comfort of your own home.

QUESTION

How does a barometer work?

EXPERIMENT OVERVIEW

You will be building your own home barometer, which will allow you to track the weather over several days and predict the weather to come. You will be using water levels in an empty 2-liter bottle to record the rise and fall of the atmospheric pressure. After you gather a few days' worth of data, you'll be able to compare your predictions to those of the local weather forecasters!

SCIENCE CONCEPT

Barometers are used to measure the air pressure outside at any given time. They can also be used to predict the weather. This requires tracking pressure values over time to determine if there is a trend toward increased pressure or toward lowered pressure.

By measuring the height of the water in your bottle due to the air pressure outside the bottle, you'll have a way to compare one day's value to another. Over time, you can use the changing heights to make your own predictions.

MATERIALS

Empty 2-liter plastic bottle (smaller bottles will work as well)   Marking pen
Fish tank   Paper
Water   Knife or scissors

PROCEDURE

1. Use a knife or scissors to cut the bottom off the plastic bottle so that it sits evenly on the table. You may need to ask for help from an adult for this step.

2. Fill the pan about half full of water.

3. With the bottom cut off of the bottle, the cap must be screwed on and, inverted, the neck of the bottle becomes the bottom when filling. Fill the bottle with enough water so that when inverted, the water level inside the bottle is above that of the pan. It will look a little like a funnel as it is filled. Then it will be inverted and placed into the pan of water. Place the bottle in the water so that it sits evenly on the bottom of the pan. Make a small mark on the bottle indicating the height of the water.

4. Take a strip of paper and make a scale with evenly marked intervals. There should be a zero point on your strip of paper, with several markings above and below that mark. You will use this to track the changing heights of the water. To accurately show the small increments that you will want to measure, make your scale fairly small, perhaps starting with markings every $\frac{1}{8}$ inch.

5. Attach your measuring scale to the side of the bottle, placing the zero point at the exact level of the water in the bottle.

6. Make one mark on your measuring scale at the beginning water level. Use your mark to indicate the date of your first measurement.

7. Wait 24 hours and measure again. Make another mark to represent your second measurement.

8. Continue measuring each day for one week. After the week has passed, take off the measuring scale, and look at your measurements.

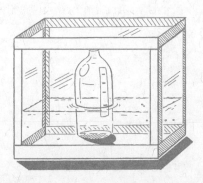

QUESTIONS FOR THE SCIENTIST

- Did the height of the water change over the week?

- Did the height go up or down?

- What kind of change in air pressure produces this kind of change in your water level?

- What kind of weather would you predict based on the change in heights?

- Did your local weather match this prediction?

Now that you have tried this experiment, you can repeat it by making more measuring scales and actually predicting the upcoming weather.

Congratulations! You are a **meteorologist!**

WORDS to KNOW

meteorologist: a person who studies and reports weather conditions.

CONCLUSION

If air pressure increases, the outside air will press down on the water in the pan and push it up into the bottle. This will produce an increase in height of the water. When weather forecasters use the term "inches of mercury," they are using a similar scale to measure the height of a different liquid due to the outside air pressure.

If the weather was pretty consistent during the course of the week, you may not have seen much change in your barometer. Don't be discouraged! Try it again, and give yourself more time. This experiment will work all year long.

MOTION

Playgrounds are fun. Whether you like swinging on a swing, climbing on the jungle gym, or riding the teeter-totter, there are plenty of fun things to do on a playground. Physics teachers love playgrounds, too, but not so much because the rides are fun. The rides you find at the playground can teach some of the most basic and important laws of physics that you can learn. What makes playgrounds so great is that you get to have lots of fun while learning!

How did the careless scientist start a war?

He invented the wheel and caused a revolution!

TRY THIS SEESAW

QUESTION
How do you balance a seesaw?

MATERIALS
Pencil
Ruler with inch markings
10 pennies, minted after 1982 (because you need them to have the same metals inside)

PROCEDURE

1. Place the pencil on a hard surface such as a table.

2. Place the ruler on the pencil so that it balances at the 6-inch mark.

3. Place five pennies at one end of the ruler.

4. Take five more pennies and find the location on the other side of the ruler that will make the ruler balance.

Science Online

Learn more about the world of physical science. Visit *www.explorescience.com*.

5. Clear the ruler off.

6. Place six pennies at the 2-inch mark on the ruler.

7. Find the location on the other side of the ruler at which only three pennies will balance the original six.

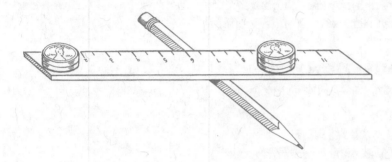

Fun Facts

Gravity on the moon is about one-sixth what it is on Earth. This means that objects fall six times faster on Earth than on the moon!

WHAT'S HAPPENING

The pencil under the ruler turns the ruler into a **lever.** The pencil acts as the fulcrum, or the balance point. To balance the ruler, there needs to be the same kind of force on one side as there is on the other. The force is **gravity,** acting on the pennies. But there's a catch! The farther away from the fulcrum the pennies are, the more their gravity counts toward balancing the ruler. For example, three pennies located 4 inches from the fulcrum (think 3 × 4 = 12) will balance six pennies located only 2 inches from the fulcrum (6 × 2 = 12). Can you think of other combinations that will balance those three pennies?[1]

FOLLOW-UP

The next time you want to ride the teeter-totter and find that your partner is much heavier than you, see if you can figure out where you both should sit. Will this work if you ride with one of your parents? If you know each other's weight, you should be able to come up with a seating arrangement that works.[2]

WORDS to KNOW

lever: a device used to lift very heavy objects.

gravity: the force that pulls us toward the center of the earth and keeps us on the ground.

TRY THIS WATER BALLOON TOSS

A fun game to play that people of all ages enjoy is the water balloon toss. From Mom and Dad's company picnic to the annual Fourth of July barbecue to kids' birthday parties, people love to see how far they can toss water balloons without breaking them. Of course, if they do break, you get wet, and that can be as fun as winning.

QUESTION

How do you keep the balloon from breaking?

MATERIALS

Several filled water balloons
A friend who doesn't mind getting wet

PROCEDURE

1. Pick up one balloon and stand facing your friend. Toss the balloon. After a successful catch, both of you take a step backward.

2. After your friend tosses the balloon back to you, each of you takes another step backward. Continue this process until the balloon breaks.

3. See how far apart you can get without breaking the balloon.

Fun Facts

A homemade water balloon launcher can send a water balloon over two football fields lengthwise.

What will you see if you drop a cup full of a hot drink?

You'll see gravi-tea (gravity) in action!

WHAT'S HAPPENING

A water balloon is simply water held by a rubber covering (the balloon). As long as nothing causes the rubber to burst, the balloon will stay intact. Pavement is hard and doesn't "give" when something collides with it, so water balloons tossed onto pavement will typically burst. Grass, on the other hand, is much softer than pavement, so balloons will often stay intact when they land on grass.

To win a water balloon contest, you apply what is known as the Impulse-Momentum Theorem—a fancy way of saying that if you give a little with your hands (move them backward as you catch the balloon), the force won't make the balloon burst.

FOLLOW-UP

Football players wear pads so that the collisions involved in tackling aren't as painful. Gymnasts and wrestlers perform on padded mats to cushion the impact. Skydivers bend their knees and sometimes run several steps when they reach the ground. Can you think of other people who use this idea of cushioning to soften a blow?[3]

_____

_____

_____

_____

_____

_____

_____

Cool Quotes

Every sentence I utter must be understood not as an affirmation, but as a question.

—Niels Bohr, Danish physicist

KIDS' LAB LESSONS

QUESTION   Why do boats float?

EXPERIMENT OVERVIEW   Using pieces of modeling clay and other simple materials, you'll be exploring how size and shape affect a boat's ability to float. You'll also get to see just how much weight your boat can hold and which design works the best.

SCIENCE CONCEPT   According to the **Archimedes Principle**, boats float because water pushes up on them with a force equal to their weight. This is called buoyancy. You can take a material (clay for example), and form it into a shape that will sink. Or you can take the same amount of clay as you had before, and form it into a boat that floats. You, and boat designers around the world, have to determine what shape produces the most buoyancy. Once you do that, you're ready to begin loading your boat with cargo.

Science Online

For answers to your questions about how stuff works, check out HowStuffWorks.com. Visit *www.howstuffworks.com.*

MATERIALS
Tank of water (aquarium) or large
    mixing bowl
Modeling clay
Pennies
Paper clips

Archimedes Principle: an object displaces its own weight in water.

PROCEDURE

1. Roll a lump of clay about the size of your palm into a ball and drop it into the water.
2. Mold the clay into several different shapes until it floats. Then place pennies in your boat until it finally sinks. Keep track of how many pennies it held.
3. Test several successful shapes to see which holds the most pennies before sinking.

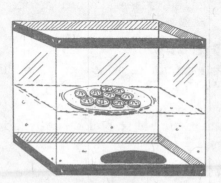

QUESTIONS FOR THE SCIENTIST

• Which clay boat held more weight? _____

• What characteristic of the winning boats helped them support the most weight?

   _____

• Does this idea apply to large ships that cross oceans and carry thousands of tons of cargo? How do they stay afloat if they are made of metal? _____

   _____

• Why don't people float like your boats did? _____

FOLLOW-UP   Another force that acts like buoyancy is air resistance. Air pushes back on falling objects in a manner similar to how water held up your boat. The project at the end of this section deals with how objects fall through the air and what effects air resistance has on their speed as they fall.

TRY THIS CORNERS

Most of what you've covered so far in this chapter has to do with gravity, but there's much more to the world of physics. Everywhere you look, objects are in motion—cars, birds, leaves, baseballs, children on a playground. Have you ever been in a car and felt pushed toward the door when the car turned? The car turns left and you are pushed to the right!

QUESTION

Why do you get pushed toward the door when the car turns?

MATERIALS

A car with an adult driving (everyone must be wearing a seatbelt!)
A road with several corners
Optional: Helium-filled balloon attached to a string

PROCEDURE

1. Have the adult make several turns at various (yet safe) speeds. Describe how you feel when the car turns and in which direction you feel pushed.

2. If you have a balloon, hold it by the string so it is free to move in the air.

3. Have the adult make several more turns and describe the motion of the balloon.

Fun Facts

Sir Isaac Newton discovered his Three Laws of Motion while in the country avoiding the spread of the plague in the 1600s in England.

WORDS to KNOW

inertia: a property of an object that makes it maintain its state of motion. That means that if it is moving, it will tend to stay moving. If it is at rest, it will stay at rest.

WHAT'S HAPPENING

You aren't actually being pushed toward the door. You possess something called **inertia**. It comes from being made of matter, and it is a little bit like your weight. Your inertia is moving in whatever direction you are, and according to a law discovered by Isaac Newton, called the Law of Inertia, it wants to keep moving in that direction. When the car turns, there's a problem. It's going in one direction and your inertia is going in another direction. The car is bigger than you are so it can make you change direction, but only by pushing on you. But this still isn't why you feel like you are being pushed toward the door. The door actually pushes on you, to make you turn! Inertia makes you feel like you're falling into the door.

FOLLOW-UP

The "door pushing on you" explanation still doesn't explain the motion of the balloon. Can you figure out why it went in the opposite direction you did?[4]

_____

_____

_____

_____

_____

_____

Around the Bend

Can you find the seven terms that have to do with the Laws of Motion? Instead of reading in a straight line, each word has one bend in it. Words can go in any direction. One word has been circled for you.

GRAVITY   FORCE
INERTIA   PHYSICS
REACTION   LEVER
ISAAC NEWTON   MOTION

```
W H Y G D L I D T H E
F A I R R E S I T U I
P N N A N V E R A Y S
H P E V I T Y H N Y A
Y S R I C I S T C C A
S R T I A O M S E C S
I C S T H F O R N E P
L A Y N O I T E C G R
R O U N D ? W T O E G
E T T O T T H E A O T
H E R N O I T C S L I
D E ! N H A H A H A !
```

TRY THIS BALLOON ROCKET

Once you have seen what causes objects to move in a certain direction, you are ready to think about how they get going in that direction in the first place. If you've ever seen a space shuttle take off, you probably noticed a huge cloud of gas and fire coming out of the back end as it lifted off. Why do rockets have to burn so much fuel to make the shuttle go?

QUESTION

How do rockets work?

MATERIALS

Latex balloon
Long string
Plastic straw
Tape

Fun Facts

It would require a helium balloon more than thirteen feet in diameter to make an 85-pound person float.

PROCEDURE

1. Blow up the balloon and hold the neck with your fingers so no air escapes.

2. Hold the balloon in front of you and let go of the neck. Observe the motion of the balloon.

3. Feed the string through the straw and attach both ends of the string to a wall or other solid support so that the straw is suspended above the floor of the room.

4. Blow up the balloon and hold the neck as before.

5. While holding the neck of the balloon, tape the balloon to the straw. Stand back and let go of the balloon. Observe the motion of the balloon.

WHAT'S HAPPENING

To make something move, there must be a force on it. While nothing appears to push on your balloon, there really is something making it move—air! When the balloon releases its air, the air particles that escape encounter other air particles outside the balloon. Each group of air particles experiences forces from the other. That is why you can feel the air coming out of the balloon. But it's also what makes the balloon move. This is an example of another Law of Motion discovered by Isaac Newton, the one commonly known as Action/Reaction. It says that every action (the air escaping and pushing on the outside air) has an equal and opposite reaction (the outside air pushing back on the air in the balloon, and making the balloon move). Rockets work in the same way, but instead of using inflated balloons, they use huge engines burning very powerful fuel.

Silly Experiments . . .

Why did the scientist take the ruler to bed?

To see how long he slept!

•

Why did the scientist put sugar under her pillow?

To see if she had sweet dreams!

•

Why did the scientist sit on her watch?

To see what it was like to be on time!

•

Why did the scientist keep a ruler in his laboratory?

To see if he could keep his facts straight!

KIDS' LAB LESSONS

QUESTION   What makes a swing go?

EXPERIMENT OVERVIEW   In this experiment you will be setting up several swinglike devices, called **pendulums,** to test what makes them swing faster and slower. You will experiment with the length of the swing, the weight hanging off the pendulum, and the size of the swing to determine which affect the time it takes to complete one full swing.

pendulum: a swinging apparatus formed by hanging a weight from the end of a long string.

period: the time it takes a pendulum to complete one full swing.

SCIENCE CONCEPT   In the 1500s in Italy, Galileo was fascinated with the swinging chandeliers in the cathedral of Pisa. In his laboratory, he set up experiments to test the factors he thought would make the chandeliers swing faster. To make the experiments as similar as possible, he used the term **period** to describe the time it took to make one complete swing—from one side across to the other and back. The three easiest factors to test are how long the pendulum is, how much weight is on the pendulum, and how large the swing is. You will have to pick one factor at a time and, while keeping the other two constant, change the factor you chose to determine whether those changes had any effect on the period.

MATERIALS

Several identical items (for example, spoons, screws, washers, pencils)

1 long (36 inches or more) piece of string

Doorway

Thumbtacks

Stopwatch

PROCEDURE

Part I: Weight

1. Tie one item to your string.
2. Attach the other end of the string to the top of the doorway with a thumbtack.
3. Pull the string back and release it at the same time you start the stopwatch.
4. Count 10 complete swings and stop the watch when the tenth swing finishes. Record the time.
5. Attach another item to your string and repeat the experiment. (This picture shows how you can hang the string at different heights.)
6. Record your time and add another item. Repeat this process of adding items until you have four times recorded.

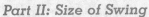

Part II: Size of Swing

1. Remove all but the first item and pull the swing back a small amount.
2. As before, count 10 complete swings and record your time.
3. Pull the swing back a little more than before and repeat the experiment. Record your time.
4. Repeat this process of pulling the swing a little farther back than before until you have four times recorded.

Part III: Length

1. Again, start with just one item and record the time for 10 swings.
2. Shorten the swing by about 4 inches.
3. Repeat the experiment, taking care to pull the swing back the same amount as before. Record your time.
4. Repeat this process of shortening the string by 4 inches until you have four times recorded.

QUESTIONS FOR THE SCIENTIST

- What factor(s) affected the period of the swing? _____

- Why do you think the other factors didn't have an effect on the period? _____

  _____

- When you swing on the playground, what do you have to do to keep from slowing down? _____

WORDS to KNOW

electricity: energy stored in positive and negative charges.

battery: a device that stores electrical energy.

Fun Facts

Some rocks are naturally magnetic. They are called lodestones and were first discovered in a region called Magnesia, near Greece.

ENERGY

Energy comes in many different forms. For example, the sun gives us energy in the form of sunlight and heat. When we eat food, we give our bodies energy so we can run and play. Cars, trains, and airplanes all have energy, too. Another form of energy is produced when we plug something into an electrical outlet in the wall.

CAUTION: Only an adult should ever plug an appliance into a wall outlet! This form of energy is called **electricity,** and it has been around for thousands of years, even though we've used it in our homes for only less than 200 years. One interesting use of electricity is to make it act like a magnet.

TRY THIS MAGNETIC ELECTRICITY

QUESTION
Can electricity confuse a compass?

MATERIALS
Small compass (used for navigation)
1 piece of insulated wire with bare wire on either end
1 **battery** (1.5 volts)

PROCEDURE

1. Lay the compass on a table so that it points to the north.

2. Place the wire across the top of the compass so that it lies in the same direction that the compass points. Leave the exposed ends of the wire outside the compass.

3. Touch each end of the wire to opposite ends of the battery. Observe what happens to the compass.

Fun Facts

The magnetic north pole (the location a compass points to) isn't located at the true North Pole. It's actually located at Ellef Ringnes Island in the Canadian arctic. It moves to the northwest approximately 15 kilometers each year.

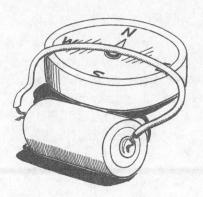

WHAT'S HAPPENING

Hans Christian Oersted discovered that electricity flowing through a wire, called a current, makes the wire act like a magnet. The magnet formed by the electricity attracts the compass, which is a very small magnet itself, and makes it point in a direction different from north.

FOLLOW-UP

Remove the wires from the battery and watch the compass return to its normal position. Now place the wire under the compass and touch the wires to the battery again. What do you see[5]?

What did one magnet say to the other magnet?

"I find you very attractive."

KIDS' LAB LESSONS

QUESTION   How does an **electromagnet** work?

EXPERIMENT OVERVIEW   In this experiment you will build your own electromagnet. By wrapping wire around a screwdriver, you will strengthen the magnetic field produced by the current flowing in the wire (which you explored in the previous experiment). Then you'll be able to measure the strength of your electromagnet by counting the number of paper clips you can hold.

SCIENCE CONCEPT   Since one wire is known to produce a magnetic field, wrapping a wire into a series of loops or coils strengthens that effect. These coils are called **solenoids;** when they are used with a metallic core (like a screwdriver), they produce surprisingly strong magnetic fields. When an ordinary nail is exposed to those fields, it, too, becomes magnetized, as long as the field is there.

WORDS to KNOW

electromagnet: a magnet made by passing electrical current through a wire.

solenoid: a cylinder of wire formed into coils.

MATERIALS
Long piece of copper wire, preferably insulated
Screwdriver
Tape
AA, C, or D battery
Paper clips

Fun Facts

Electromagnets differ from permanent magnets in that they can be turned on and off.

PROCEDURE

1. Leaving about 3 inches of one end of the wire free, wrap the wire around the screwdriver 10 times.
2. Tape one end of the wire to the negative terminal (marked with a "–") of the battery.
3. Hold the handle of the screwdriver in one hand while you touch the free end of the wire to the positive terminal (marked with a "+") of the battery.
4. See how many paper clips you can pick up and hold with the screwdriver.
5. Remove the free wire from the battery and wind another 10 loops around the screwdriver.
6. Repeat the experiment and count the number of paper clips you can pick up.
7. Again, remove the free wire from the battery.
8. Wind any remaining wire around the screwdriver, leaving about 3 inches of wire free and repeat the experiment.

QUESTIONS FOR THE SCIENTIST

• What made the screwdriver turn into a magnet? _____

_____

• How did you turn the electromagnet on and off? _____

• What effect did adding more coils to the screwdriver have on the number of paper clips you could pick up? _____

• What advantages might there be to using a magnet that can be turned on and off? _____

FOLLOW-UP   Practice lifting paper clips, moving them through the air, and then dropping them in another location. Can you think of anywhere someone would want to do this?[6] _____

_____

WORDS to KNOW

afterimage: what we see in our eyes even after we stop looking at an object.

Cool Quotes

The sun, with all those planets revolving around it and dependent on it, can still ripen a bunch of grapes as if it had nothing else in the universe to do.

—Galileo

TRY THIS BIRD CAGE

Energy exists in forms other than electricity. Look around—do you see colors? If so, you are receiving light energy that was produced in the sun, traveled more than 90 million miles to Earth, bounced off the objects you are looking at, and reflected into your eyes. Amazing! Light and color are examples of energy we see around us every day but we sometimes forget to notice.

QUESTION

What is an **afterimage**?

MATERIALS

Scissors
3" × 5" note card
Colored pens
Tape
Pencil

PROCEDURE

1. Cut the note card in half.

2. On one of the pieces, draw a picture of a bird in the middle of the card.

3. On the other piece, draw a cage, also in the middle of the card.

4. Tape each card, back to back, to the end of the pencil so you can see one picture on either side.

5. Rub the pencil very quickly between your palms until you have captured the bird in the cage.

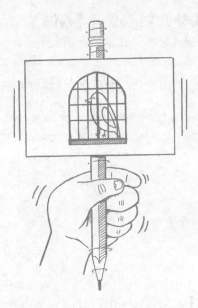

WHAT'S HAPPENING

Your eyes have the ability to see images even after they are gone. These are called after-images. When you spin the pencil fast enough, your eyes still see the cage while the bird comes into view, and it appears as though the bird is actually inside the cage. The same happens when the bird spins out of view. You still see it while the cage is visible, and the bird appears to be caught in the cage.

FOLLOW-UP

Try making other drawings for your afterimage viewer. Try flowers and a vase, a person on a swing, or even a face on the moon. You can use colors to make the images appear even more realistic.

Catchy Categories

An important part of the Scientific Method is putting things into categories. Take the words in the following list and group them into two categories. Complete each criss-cross grid with the words that fit the given category. HINT: We left you a L-I-S-T in each grid to help you get started.

WORD LIST:
fast
solid
slow
gravity
liquid
speed
gas
swing
balance
weight
inertia
mass
density
force
fall
size

Properties of Motion

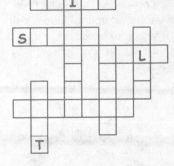

Properties of Matter

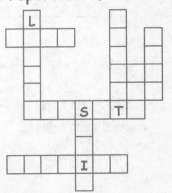

WORDS to KNOW

filter: a way to block certain colors of light from reaching your eyes.

Science Online

The EncycloZine has a collection of fascinating optical illusions. Visit *www.encyclozine.com*. From the main page, click on "Optical Illusions."

Where does a mad scientist go to college?

A looney-versity!

TRY THIS COLORS OF LIGHT

Color is a pretty interesting topic to study. In school, you probably learned to mix colors to make new colors. For example, green is made by mixing blue and yellow, and purple is made by mixing blue and red. In fact, every color can be made from the right combination of the three primary colors: red, yellow, and blue. But has anyone ever tried to convince you that red, blue, and yellow aren't the only primary colors? They aren't.

QUESTION

What are the primary colors of light?

MATERIALS

Cellophane or plastic squares large enough to cover the light end of the flashlight. You will need 1 each of red, blue, and green.
3 flashlights
Rubber bands
A white screen or wall

PROCEDURE

1. Secure one square of cellophane or plastic to the end of each flashlight with a rubber band.

2. Turn on each flashlight to make sure it produces the correct color of light.

3. Carefully shine the red and blue lights onto the screen so that the color circles overlap. What color is produced?

4. Shine the red and green lights onto the screen. What color is produced by this pair of colors?

5. Shine the blue and green lights onto the screen. What color is produced by this pair of colors?

6. Carefully shine all three lights onto the screen so that all three colors overlap in the middle. What color is produced by all three colors?

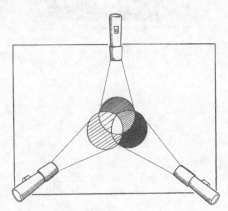

WHAT'S HAPPENING

Light behaves differently than paint does. Red, blue, and green can combine to form every color of light, so they are called primary. Secondary colors are formed when two primary colors are mixed. These were the first three colors you produced: magenta, yellow, and cyan (blue). When you shined all three colors onto the screen, you should have produced white light. If your cellophane covers weren't totally pure (most aren't), you may have seen an off-white color.

FOLLOW-UP

Try looking at the world through the red, blue, or green **filters**. You will probably notice that most of what you see is the color of the filter you are looking through. But you may also see some objects that look black. The light from these objects is being blocked by your filter, so you see no color.

Black and White

Can you find the figure that is the EXACT opposite of the three figures in the box below? Draw a line between each pair.

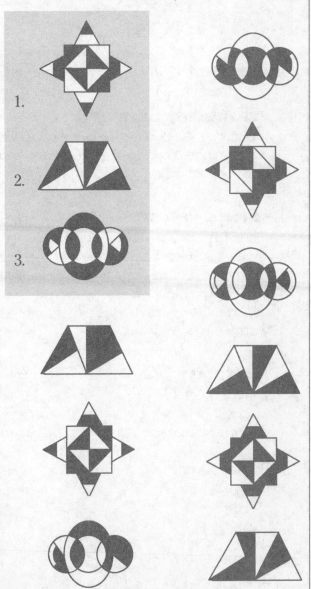

1.

2.

3.

KIDS' LAB LESSONS

QUESTION   Which color is hotter: black or white?

EXPERIMENT OVERVIEW   In this experiment you'll be testing to see whether a black object heats up faster than a white object. You'll test the temperature of water inside a can of each color and also test the temperature of the air under a card of each color.

SCIENCE CONCEPT   Each color of light that we see reaches our eyes because it has reflected off another object. All the other colors of light that hit that object were absorbed. Some objects absorb more light than others. In fact, white objects must reflect all the light they receive, which means they don't absorb any. On the other hand, black objects reflect no light to our eyes, which means they absorb all the light they receive. This experiment will show which of these two ends up being warmer.

MATERIALS
2 thermometers
2 sheets of paper: 1 white and 1 black
2 tin cans: 1 painted white and 1 painted black (have an adult help you paint
    the cans)
Pitcher of water

PROCEDURE

1. Place the thermometers outside and lay one sheet of paper over each one.
2. Let them sit for 30 minutes.
3. Remove the papers and compare the temperature each thermometer shows.
4. Fill each can with water at the same temperature and place the corresponding sheet of paper on top to cover it (black on black, white on white).
5. Set both cans outside for 30 minutes. Remove the papers and compare the temperature of each can of water.

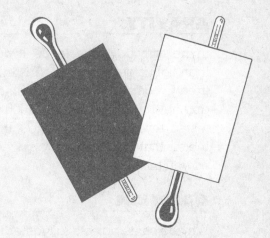

QUESTIONS FOR THE SCIENTIST

• Which thermometer measured a higher temperature in the first experiment?

_____

_____

• Which can of water was warmest? _____

_____

_____

• On a cold day, which color would be better to wear to school—black or white?

_____

_____

• If you lived in a very hot place, what color car would you buy if you wanted to stay as cool as possible? _____

_____

SCIENCE FAIR PROJECT: PHYSICS

GRAVITY

In the early days of science, it was generally accepted that heavier objects fell faster than light objects. In fact, Aristotle, a famous scientist during the fourth century B.C., tried to come up with a mathematical relationship between the weight of the object and how fast it fell. Nearly 2,000 years later, Galileo didn't think that was right. He tested several objects, without the technology we now have, and decided that it was the air that made certain objects fall more slowly than others, not their weight. What do you think?

QUESTION

Why do some objects fall faster than others?

EXPERIMENT OVERVIEW

In this experiment you'll be testing several objects to see what features determine how fast they fall. You'll be picking heavy and light objects, large and small objects, solid and hollow objects, and you'll drop them all. You will then be able to scientifically determine what makes one object fall faster than another.

SCIENCE CONCEPT

Long ago, people generally believed that the heavier something was, the faster it would fall through the air. The person most famous for holding this belief was named Aristotle. Today, we have plenty of examples that back that claim up. For example, if you were in a helicopter and you dropped a Ping-Pong ball and a bowling ball out of the door at the same time, the bowling ball would hit the ground first. But since Ping-Pong balls and bowling balls aren't the same size, try another example. Drop a Ping-Pong ball and a golf ball and the Ping-Pong ball still loses. So what's the big deal?

   In the 1500s, a man named Galileo tried to show that it really didn't matter how much an object weighed—that it would usually fall at the same speed as any other object, as long as you didn't have to take air into account. You've already looked at a few experiments about air and there are more to come, but for now, think about the effect air has on a falling object.

When you run down the street or open the window in your car, you feel the wind. If it's strong enough, it can make it hard to walk or run. Now imagine that you are falling through the air. The faster you go, the windier it feels and the harder it becomes to move. A heavier person wouldn't be affected as much as a light person would be. That is the idea of air resistance, and you'll explore it in this experiment.

MATERIALS

1 object you would call "light"—e.g., feather

1 object you would call "heavy"—e.g., rock

1 object you would call "small"—e.g., plastic figurine

1 object you would call "large"—e.g., basketball

1 object you would call "solid"—e.g., croquet ball

1 object you would call "hollow"—e.g., Wiffle ball

4 other objects of your choice

1 sheet of paper

1 writing utensil

A platform or raised place from which you can drop these items. (The higher you can climb the better, but you must be sure that the area below is open and free of people. Dropping objects can be very dangerous.)

A partner who can tell you which object lands first

PROCEDURE

You will be recording results from each test. An example is shown below:

Test: Light (object name, e.g., feather) vs. Heavy (object name, e.g., rock)

Light object (feather)—small, white, weighs almost nothing, about 3 inches long, not solid

Heavy object (rock)—medium sized, brown and black, weighs about the same as a baseball, about 3 inches in diameter, round, solid

Winner: The rock

1. In order, test the following pairs and record your results:
   Light—heavy
   Small—large
   Solid—hollow
   Other pairings from your collection of objects

2. When you have finished testing, look at the results and determine the factors that made objects fall the fastest.

QUESTIONS FOR THE SCIENTIST

- Of your entire collection, which object fell the fastest?

- Which characteristics of this object made it fall fast?

- Which characteristics had no effect on how fast it fell?

- Which object fell the slowest?

- Which pairing showed the most significant differences in how fast the objects fell?

- What could you do to eliminate air from this experiment so you could test Galileo's claim?

CONCLUSION

The shape of the object is a very important factor in how fast it falls. It's true that weight matters too—really light objects fall slowly no matter how they are shaped because once they start hitting the air, they immediately slow down. But the heavier the object, the more its shape matters. A simple test to verify this result is to drop a single sheet of notebook paper at the same time you drop a crumpled up piece of the same paper. Try it and you'll see the difference shape makes.

Modern science has shown us that if we take away air, objects will fall at the same speed no matter how big or small they are and no matter what shape they are. When the astronauts went to the moon, they dropped a feather and a hammer to see which would fall faster. On the moon, there is no air. (Astronauts wear special suits to help them breathe.) Can you guess what happened? The feather and hammer landed at the same time.

CHAPTER 4
THE PLANET EARTH

Why did the poor scientist experiment with baking bread?

Because he needed the dough!

Fun Facts

Much of the acid rain in North America is caused by the burning of coal to produce electricity.

The rainiest day ever recorded was in 1952 in Cilaos, Reunion Island. In a 24-hour period, 73.63 inches of rain fell.

WORDS to KNOW

acid rain: rain that contains acids formed in the clouds. It can be dangerous to people, animals, and crops.

Do you ever have one of those days when you lay down in the grass, feel the warm sun all around you, look up at the clouds moving past, and wonder how it all happened? The earth is in many ways a miracle. Nowhere else in the entire universe has anyone discovered a place where life can exist. Sure there are other stars like our sun, and now scientists are discovering planets that orbit those stars. But so far, no one has found water, trees, grass, and a climate quite like ours here on Earth.

The planet Earth is a rare find in the universe, and it is in our care. If we don't take care of it, its wonder and beauty may soon be in danger. One of the growing concerns among people who are worried about the earth is the quality of our air and water. There are many ways to discover how precious these resources are.

TRY THIS ACID RAIN

QUESTION
What is acid rain?

MATERIALS
Empty glass jar
Water
Phenol red (available at pool supply stores)
A drinking straw

PROCEDURE

1. Fill the jar about half to three-quarters full of cool water.

2. Put approximately 20 drops of the phenol red into the water until it turns light red. You can practice this and adjust the amount you add, once you get the hang of the experiment.

3. Place the straw into the water and blow so that bubbles form in the water for about 20 seconds. CAUTION: Do not drink the water!

4. Check the color of the water. It should be a lighter red than it was before.

5. Repeat your 20 seconds of blowing a few more times. Before long, the water should be clear again.

WHAT'S HAPPENING

Phenol red reacts with acids to change color. (You have already learned a little bit about acids in an earlier chapter.) When you blew into the water, the carbon dioxide you blew out (which is not the same as the oxygen you breathe in) reacted with the tap water to form a very weak acid. The more you blew, the more the acid reacted with the phenol red and turned the water clear. Pool cleaners use phenol red to measure how acidic the water is. This tells them what kinds of chemicals to add to maintain the cleanliness of the water.

FOLLOW-UP

What does this have to do with acid rain? When we place too much carbon dioxide into

Wind Speed

How fast can you find 20 words that are hidden in the word ANEMOMETER (a device that measures wind speed)? Each word must be three letters or longer.

Extra Experiment: Use a separate piece of paper and see if you can come up with: 20 four-letter words, 5 five-letter words, and 4 six-letter words. If you are a SUPER scientist, you will even be able to make 1 seven-letter word!

_____ _____

_____ _____

_____ _____

_____ _____

_____ _____

_____ _____

_____ _____

_____ _____

_____

the air, through burning coal, gasoline, or other fossil fuels, it can react with the water in the air (rainwater) to form an acid. When that rain falls to the ground, we get acid in our water and it can become unsafe. It pays to be careful with the gases we exhaust into the air!

KIDS' LAB LESSONS

Winds follow a pattern across the face of the earth, called the Coriolis effect. This pattern tends to produce winds that rotate in a counter-clockwise direction in the Northern **Hemisphere** and in a clockwise direction in the Southern Hemisphere.

QUESTION   How can you tell how fast the wind is blowing?

EXPERIMENT OVERVIEW   In this experiment you will build a simple **anemometer**, a device that measures wind speed. While you won't actually be able to come up with the true wind speed for this project, you'll be able to track different speeds on your own scale and identify which days were the windiest.

SCIENCE CONCEPT   Breezes constantly blow across the surface of the earth, and only rarely do they reach the point of being dangerous to people. An anemometer catches the wind in small cups that then rotate. The faster the cups rotate, the faster the wind is blowing.

WORDS to KNOW

hemisphere: half of the earth.

anemometer: a device that measures wind speed.

MATERIALS
Glue
Empty spool of thread
  or lump of modeling clay
Small block of wood
Pencil
Needle or thin nail
Stopwatch

1 large piece of sturdy
  cardboard
Scissors
Stapler
Foil muffin cups
1 bright sticker

PROCEDURE

1. Glue the spool of thread to the block of wood and wedge the pencil, eraser side up, into it.
2. Stick the needle into the eraser.
3. Cut two strips out of the piece of cardboard. They should be at least 16 inches long and 2 inches wide.
4. With the scissors, cut slits in the bottom of each strip so they fit together to make a cross. Start from the middle of the strip (about 8 inches from either side) and cut upward about 1 inch.
5. Glue or staple one muffin cup to each arm of the cross, making sure that each cup points in the same direction. This will ensure that every cup will catch the wind.
6. Place the sticker on one of the cups. Make sure it is clearly visible because you will be using it to measure wind speed.
7. Place the cross onto the needle so that it rotates freely. If you find that it doesn't rotate, use the needle to make a slightly larger hole until it spins easily.
8. Place the anemometer outdoors where it can catch the wind.
9. Over the course of several days record the wind speed at different times of day.

Fun Facts

Winds are measured on the Beaufort scale, which ranges from 0 (no wind) to 12 (hurricane speeds in excess of 75 mph).

The fastest wind recorded on the ground was 231 mph in New Hampshire in 1934.

Instructions on Measuring Wind Speed Use a stopwatch or a clock that will measure one minute. Count the number of times the cup with the sticker completes one revolution in a minute. Use that number as your wind speed. Each time you record a new measurement, compare it to the previous values.

QUESTIONS FOR THE SCIENTIST

- What was the fastest speed you recorded? _____

- What time of day was the windiest? The calmest?_____

- Are there places at your house that are windier than others? How could you test this? _____

- How do you suppose meteorologists measure the true wind speed?[1] _____

Fun Facts

The world's most active region for volcanoes lies in what is called the Ring of Fire, a circular region extending around the Pacific Ocean from East Asia to the United States.

WORDS to KNOW

volcano: any part of the earth (especially mountains) that explodes when pressure below it gets too high.

molten: melted.

Science Online

The U.S. Geological Services Cascade Volcano Observatory (CVO) includes links to all of the world's known volcanoes. Visit *http://vulcan.wr.usgs.gov*.

TRY THIS MINI VOLCANO

QUESTION

What does an erupting volcano look like?

MATERIALS

Small plastic bottle
Baking soda
Wide tray or baking pan
Sand or dirt

½ cup vinegar
Measuring cup with a pouring lip
Red food coloring

PROCEDURE:

1. Fill the bottle one-quarter to half full of baking soda and place it in the middle of the tray.
2. Pile the sand around the bottle so that you can just see the opening. At this point it should look like a small volcano.
3. Pour the vinegar into the measuring cup.
4. Place several drops of food coloring into your vinegar and quickly pour it into the bottle top.

WHAT'S HAPPENING

You've already seen what kind of reaction occurs when baking soda and vinegar are combined. The red coloring makes this reaction appear to produce lava. In real volcanoes, you wouldn't find any vinegar, but you would find hot gases and liquid rocks under intense pressure. When the pressure builds up too much, the volcano explodes, and all the hot gases and rocks that have melted under the heat finally burst forth in the form of either hot ash or **molten** lava.

Head in the Clouds

Do you ever see the shapes of people or animals when you look at the clouds? Connect the numbered dots and then the lettered dots to see what familiar shape is floating overhead in this beautiful sky. HINT: To make a better cloud picture, connect the dots with curved lines instead of straight lines.

TRY THIS LAND WARMER

From the dirt in our gardens to the liquid metal core of our planet, the earth is a place where remarkable processes happen every day without our knowledge. One of the simplest processes is the manner in which sunlight warms our planet.

QUESTION

Which gets warm faster: land or water?

MATERIALS

2 small cups
Water
Dirt
2 thermometers

PROCEDURE

1. Fill one cup with water and the other with dirt.

2. Place both cups in the freezer for 10 minutes.

3. Remove both cups from the freezer and place a thermometer in each. Record the initial temperatures.

4. Place both cups in full sunlight for a period of 15 minutes.

5. After 15 minutes, record both temperatures.

Fun Facts

Earthquakes are measured on the Richter scale—a scale where every number represents an earthquake that is 10 times more powerful than the previous number. The largest earthquakes ever recorded occurred in Colombia in 1906 and in Japan in 1933. Both measured 8.9 on the Richter scale.

Where do scientists study volcanoes?

In the lava-tory!

WHAT'S HAPPENING

Sunlight warms the land much faster than it does water. That is why your cup of dirt ended up warmer than the cup of water. This also explains why, on a hot day, a sandy beach can get extremely warm while the water in the lake remains cool.

FOLLOW-UP

When you dig in the sand on a beach, does the sand feel warm all the way down, or is it only the top level that gets hot?[2] Some animals dig into the earth to find cool places to make their nests. Can you find animals that do that?

_____
_____
_____
_____

Cool Quotes

Space isn't remote at all. It's only an hour's drive away if your car could go straight up.

—Sir Fred Hoyle, British mathematician and astronomer

Up or Down?

What is a good way to remember the difference between a stalactite and a stalagmite? Use words from the word list to finish the following "science saying," and you'll never forget which is which!

Word List
MIGHTY
STALACTITE
STALAGMITE
TIGHT

A _stalactite_

hangs _Tight_ to the ceiling.

A _stalagmite_

grows _mighty_ tall from the floor.

KIDS' LAB LESSONS

QUESTION   How do icicles grow?

EXPERIMENT OVERVIEW   In this experiment, you'll explore the formation of icicles by building **stalactites** and **stalagmites**—towers of rock-hard minerals usually found in caves deep in the earth. Surprisingly, the process by which they form is very similar to how icicles form. You'll be using a common drugstore product called Epsom salts and you'll get to watch the "icicles" grow right before your very eyes.

SCIENCE CONCEPT   Icicles can form only under special conditions. It must be cold enough for water to freeze, but there must also be a way for ice to melt so it drips. This is why icicles are commonly found along the edge of the roof of a house. The warmth of the house can cause snow on the roof to melt and drip to the edge of the house. As the water drips off the side, some of it freezes. Later, drops run down the frozen droplets and freeze when they reach the end. In this fashion, the icicle grows drop by drop.

In caves, stalactites and stalagmites grow in the same way. The only difference is that the water that drips doesn't freeze. Instead, each drop of water leaves behind a tiny amount of calcite, which hardens on the end of the stalactite. Eventually, enough calcite builds up and hardens that a stalactite forms. Stalagmites are formed when some of the calcite falls to the ground and gradually builds up from the floor. After a long time, the stalactites that grow from the ceiling meet up with the stalagmites growing up from the floor until they join and a **column** is formed.

WORDS to KNOW

stalactite: a long, thin piece of hanging mineral (like rock) that forms over long periods of time, often in caves.

stalagmite: a long, thin piece of mineral that grows up from the ground over long periods of time. (It is similar to a stalactite.)

column: what is formed when a stalactite meets a stalagmite and the two grow together.

Fun Facts

It can take up to 4,000 years for a stalactite to grow 1 inch.

MATERIALS

Large glass that you can use for mixing
Water
Small spoon
Box of Epsom salts (available at a local drugstore)

2 small glasses
Thick string or a piece of cloth that will absorb water easily
Wax paper

PROCEDURE

1. Fill the large glass with water and stir in the Epsom salts until you cannot dissolve any more (some of the salt remains and won't dissolve).
2. Fill each small glass with half of the solution you have prepared and place the jars on a piece of wax paper.
3. Place an end of the string in each glass and let the middle of the string hang between the glasses.
4. Watch your stalactite and stalagmite grow over the next few days.

QUESTIONS FOR THE SCIENTIST

• Which of your cones is the stalactite and which is the stalagmite? _____

• How fast did your stalactite grow (how many inches per day)? _____
• Did the process speed up at all during your experiment? _____

• If you live where it's cold enough for icicles, how do you suppose they form?

_____

• How could you prevent icicles from forming on your house? _____

_____

FOLLOW-UP

Do you think this experiment will work with other substances? Try baking soda, table salt, sugar, and so on. Considering the fact that Epsom salts is found in drugstores, can you find other uses for it?[3]

Science Online

These links below will take you into the world of astronomy and will help you learn more about the planets and stars:

Visit *Astronomy* magazine at www.astronomy.com

Visit *Sky and Telescope* magazine at www.skyandtelescope.com

Visit the Star Gazer home page at www.jackstargazer.com

Visit The Astronomy Café at http://itss.raytheon.com/cafe/qadir/qanda.html

THE SKY ABOVE US

If you have ever looked up at the sky on a clear night, you have seen more stars than you can count. It gives you some sense of how large our universe is and might even make you feel like Earth is pretty small. Looking at the sky is one of the oldest activities known to man. Just about every ancient civilization had its own myths about what the stars mean. The passing of days, months, and years has long been tracked by the rising and setting of the sun, the phases of the moon, and the changing of the seasons.

The sky is blue and sunsets are red because of the way air breaks sunlight into colors. That fact alone is pretty fascinating. But for many of us, it's hard to imagine that air is made up of anything. You can't see it, you can't taste it, and you can only feel it when it moves. It makes you wonder whether air is really there like everyone says it is.

TRY THIS SPACE OF AIR

QUESTION
Does air take up space?

MATERIALS
Balloon (minimum 9 inches)
Glass bottle with a small mouth
Pot of boiling water
Pot of ice water

Funnel
Masking tape
Water

PROCEDURE

1. Place the mouth of the balloon over the mouth of the bottle. It should hang limply at the side of the bottle.

2. Make sure the balloon makes a good seal around the top of the bottle and gently place the bottle into the pot of boiling water. Be careful not to stand too close to the boiling water. Observe the changes in the balloon.

3. Remove the bottle from the hot water, remove the balloon, then replace it over the mouth of the bottle. The bottle now contains very hot air.

4. Place the bottle into the pot of ice water and observe the changes in the balloon.

5. Remove the bottle from the water and let it sit at room temperature for 10 minutes.

6. Remove the balloon from the top of the bottle.

7. Place the funnel in the mouth of the bottle and tape the mouth of the bottle to the funnel so that no air can escape.

8. Pour water into the funnel and watch what it does.

WHAT'S HAPPENING

Air definitely takes up space! When you first put the balloon on the bottle, you "captured" the air that was in the bottle. It didn't inflate the balloon because it fit nicely into the bottle. When you heated it up, however, the air expanded and took up even more room. The only place it could go was into the balloon, so the balloon inflated. When you removed the bottle from the hot water and placed it into the ice water, the air was compressed. Not only did it *not* inflate the balloon, it pulled the balloon down into the bottle. When you returned the bottle to its original temperature, the balloon should have returned to its original size, shape, and location.

The funnel experiment shows that air takes up room and can't easily be squeezed. When you sealed the top of the bottle, you gave the air nowhere to go. So when you poured the water into the funnel, it wasn't heavy enough to compress the air in the bottle and it remained in the funnel, apparently defying gravity.

FOLLOW-UP

Can you think of other examples of air expanding or contracting that you might encounter?[4]

_____

_____

_____

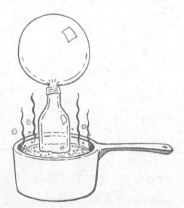

KIDS' LAB LESSONS

QUESTION   How can you use the sun to tell time?

EXPERIMENT OVERVIEW   In this experiment you'll get to build your own **sundial**. With it, you can keep time the way ancient civilizations did. As the sun rises and sets, it makes shadows of different lengths and angles. You'll use the location of the sun's shadow on your sundial to tell you exactly what time it is.

SCIENCE CONCEPT   The sun doesn't actually move around the earth; it only seems that way. Instead, the earth rotates on its axis, so at any one time about half the people on Earth can see the sun and the other half cannot. This is how we get night and day. What a sundial does is track the location of the shadow that the sun makes, and it uses that location to determine the time of day. You have to know a few things in order for your sundial to work. For example, you need to know where true north is, and you need to know where the sun's shadow will be at certain times of day. Once you have set up your sundial, you should find it to be pretty accurate!

WORDS to KNOW

sundial: an ancient time-telling device.

MATERIALS
Sturdy paper plate
Unsharpened pencil
Modeling clay
Compass
Marking pen

PROCEDURE

1. Poke a hole in the middle of the paper plate large enough for the pencil to fit through.
2. Stick the pencil through the plate. Make sure the bottom of the plate is facing up.
3. Place the end of the pencil in a lump of clay below the plate to anchor it down.
4. Use the compass to locate true north and place your sundial in an open space with the pencil pointing slightly to the north. (This method works for anyone who lives in the Northern Hemisphere. If you live in the Southern Hemisphere, you will point the pencil to the south.)
5. At 8:00 in the morning, mark on the sundial the location of the pencil's shadow. Label it "8:00 A.M." Repeat this step every two hours until sunset. Your sundial is ready!

QUESTIONS FOR THE SCIENTIST

- Are the markings evenly spaced? _____

- Do you think it matters what time of the year you build or use your sundial? What happens when the days get longer or shorter? _____

- At what time of day does the shadow of the sun point true north? Is it this way all year round? _____

FOLLOW-UP   Research some of the civilizations that used sundials and think about these questions:
- What were some of the variations they built?
- Were any of them like yours?
- Why do you think people stopped using sundials?

Look around your town to see of you can find any sundials. Check the accuracy of any you find.

Fun Facts

The earth is actually farther from the sun in the summer (94.6 million miles in June) than in the winter (91.4 million miles in December).

The earth is tilted at an angle of 23° from vertical. This is why we have seasons.

tilt of the earth: the angle the north and south poles of the earth make with a vertical line.

TRY THIS SEASONS IN THE SUN

Another way of measuring time is to mark the changing seasons. From the heat of summer, to cool crisp days in autumn when the leaves fall, to the snows of winter, to the first blooms of spring, seasons show us that time is passing and that we are indeed making our way around the sun. It's a journey that takes a full year to complete. Many people believe that the reason why it is warm in the summer and cold in the winter is because the earth is so much closer to the sun in the summer than in the winter. However, this isn't so.

QUESTION
Why do we have seasons?

MATERIALS
Marking pen
Medium or large Styrofoam ball, available at a craft supply store
Desk lamp without a shade
Pencil or long knitting needle

PROCEDURE

1. Mark the top and bottom of the ball with the letters *N* (on top) and *S* (on the bottom). These marks indicate the north and south poles.

2. Draw a circle around the middle of the ball to indicate the equator of the earth.

3. Place the lamp in the middle of your room.

4. Push the pencil through the N and S markings on the ball and tilt the top of the ball slightly toward the lamp.

5. Turn the light on and notice what parts of the ball are illuminated. This represents the beginning of summer in the Northern Hemisphere (location I).

6. Notice which wall of the room the ball is tilted toward. You will want to keep the ball tilted toward the same wall throughout the experiment. Move to a position 90° away from your starting position (location II). Again, notice what parts of the ball are illuminated. This represents the first day of fall in the Northern Hemisphere.

7. Now move another 90° around the lamp and again notice what parts of the ball are illuminated (location III). This is the beginning of winter in the Northern Hemisphere.

8. Finally, move another 90° around the lamp and note the illuminated parts of the ball (location IV). This is the first day of spring in the Northern Hemisphere.

WHAT'S HAPPENING

We have seasons with longer and shorter days not because the earth is any closer to the sun, but because of the **tilt of the earth.** When the north is tilted toward the sun, the Northern Hemisphere has summer. Days are longer and warmer and you can see this effect if you rotate the ball and notice how long the northern parts of the earth are illuminated. In the Southern Hemisphere, however, little sun reaches the ball. Days are shorter and colder and this is when they have winter. Six months later (location III), the north has winter and the south has summer. You can see how the tilt of the earth gives the south much more sunlight and how the north gets little. In spring and fall, days are about the same length all over the earth. You can see this in locations II and IV.

Sneaky Scientists

Two scientists want to arrange a secret meeting to discuss a new solar energy experiment. Use the sundial decoder to figure out the message that one scientist sent to the other. Write the secret message on the lines provided.

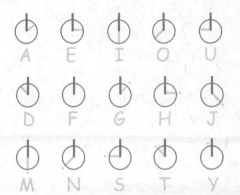

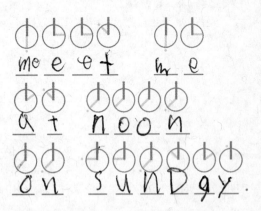

meet me
at noon
on SuNDay.

KIDS' LAB LESSONS

If you look into the sky a little beyond the sun, you'll see thousands of stars. Some of the stars appear to be connected with other stars, as if they formed a particular shape. In fact, ancient civilizations believed that the shapes formed by stars meant something, and they made up stories about the shapes. The shapes are called **constellations.** Can you find some of the more common ones?[5]

QUESTION   Why do we see only part of the moon?

EXPERIMENT OVERVIEW   In this experiment, you'll set up a model of the sun, the moon, and the earth and track the **phases of the moon** through drawings and a hands-on activity.

SCIENCE CONCEPT   Surprisingly, the same half of the moon always faces Earth. We can never see the "dark side of the moon" except from a spaceship. The only reason we can see the moon is because light from the sun reflects off its surface and back to our eyes.

As the moon orbits the earth (a journey that takes about 29 days), half of it always faces the sun. However, it isn't always the same half! So as the moon travels around the earth, we see any amount from 0 percent of the side that faces us to 100 percent of that side. These percentages are called the phases of the moon.

Formally, the phases are labeled as new moon (we can't see it), first quarter (we see the right half), full moon (we see the entire face), and third quarter (we see the left

WORDS to KNOW

constellation: any arrangement of stars in the sky into a familiar shape or pattern.

phases of the moon: the different portions of the moon that we can see during its orbit around the earth.

half). Every once in a while, the moon during its "new" phase crosses the line between the sun and the earth and we experience a solar eclipse. Not as rare are lunar eclipses, when, during the moon's "full" phase, the earth passes between the sun and the moon and casts a shadow on the moon.

MATERIALS

Current newspaper
Paper plate
Marking pen
Desk lamp as bright as possible, without a shade
Small ball, a little larger than your hand
Clean sheet of paper
Time (This experiment will take up to a month to complete, but only requires a few minutes each day.)

PROCEDURE

1. Check in your local paper to find the date of the new moon. Start your experiment on this day.
2. On the paper plate, draw marks around the outer edge representing 28 days. You might want to draw lines that cut your plate in quarters and make seven marks per quarter of the circle. You will use this as your guide for locating the ball when you begin your experiment. Start at 0/28 and begin numbering in a counter-clockwise direction.
3. Set your lamp on the side of your room against one wall. Make sure this is a location you can easily keep the lamp or place it each day for your test.
4. Turn off the light in your room and turn on the lamp.

(continued on next page)

(continued from previous page)

5. Set the plate on the floor in the middle of your room and stand on it. Point Day 0/28 toward the lamp.

6. Face in the direction of the day you are recording (beginning at Day 0 and counting upward for 28 days) and hold your ball at arm's length.

7. Take a close look at the illumination of the ball. For Day 0, there should be no illumination, as this corresponds to the new moon.

8. Record the ball's illumination on your sheet of paper in a table that allows you to track the phases of the moon over the course of one month.

9. Repeat this step each day for 28 days. When you finish, you should have 29 drawings (Day 0 through Day 28) showing the phases of the moon.

10. Periodically, check your results with the actual moon outside at night.

QUESTIONS FOR THE SCIENTIST

- Did your drawings match the actual phases of the moon? _____

_____

- What effect did the fact that the moon's orbit is actually a little longer than 28 days have on the accuracy of your data? _____

_____

- What does the fact that solar and lunar eclipses are rare tell you about the orbit of the moon? Think about how this would look in your experiment. _____

_____

FOLLOW-UP   Research the history of man's attempts to fly to the moon. What objects were left on the moon by those who visited? For a powerful look at a failed moon voyage that almost cost three astronauts their lives, rent the movie *Apollo 13.*

Fun Facts

The moon actually looks a reddish color during a lunar eclipse due to sunlight passing through the earth's atmosphere and being bent toward the moon—in effect, a "sunset" during an eclipse.

Giant Science Kriss-Kross

How can you find the answers to these science questions? If you've looked through all the chapters in this book, you will have no problem! Fill each answer into the numbered grid. The words in the shaded row will answer this riddle: **What is the best part about being a scientist?** We left you a few A-T-O-M-S to get you started. Need more help? Check out the Experiment Overviews.

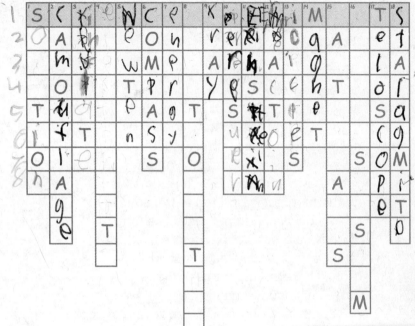

Clues:

1. A mixture of two or more liquids.
2. Animals use _____ to blend into their surroundings.
3. When you heat air in a bottle, you can _____ a balloon.
4. Scientists use this form of energy to light up their laboratories. You use it at home, too!
5. Isaac _____ is the scientist who defined the laws of gravity.
6. A _____ points toward the magnetic north.
7. The sun gives us _____ in the form of heat and light.
8. A process that uses one metal to coat another metal.
9. An _____ is a picture that shows you the inside of your body.
10. Barometers are devices used to measure air _____.

11. Albert _____ is a scientist whose theories and experiments led to new ways of thinking about time, space, matter, energy, and gravity!
12. One of the Laws of Motion says that every action has an equal but opposite _____.
13. _____ only form when it is cold enough for water to freeze, but at the same time there is a way for water to drip.
14. Electricity flowing through a wire turns the wire into an electro_____.
15. A seismologist is a scientist who uses a Ricter Scale to measure the strength of _____.
16. The _____ _____ (2 words) controls all the actions and reactions of the body.
17. An astronomer is a scientist who uses a _____ to look at the stars and planets.
18. A _____ grows up from the ground.

RIVERS

Think about the last time you looked at a river—really looked at it. Was it straight, or did it bend and curve, and maybe even wind its way through town? The more you look at rivers, the more you might wonder why they aren't straight. They start in the mountains and run to the sea. It sounds like a simple path, one that they should have carved out early in their lives and never deviated from. However, the paths of rivers have surprised and intrigued people for thousands of years. When a time of flooding comes to an area, the path of the river becomes a topic for even more discussion. It's almost like a river has a mind of its own!

QUESTION

Why aren't rivers straight?

EXPERIMENT OVERVIEW

In this experiment, you'll first get to build a mountain. To do that, you're going to need some mountain supplies and a pretty open space for the water to flow out. You're also going to need plenty of water, so plan ahead. You'll have two options to choose from, in terms of the "rain" that falls: steady or occasional. Each pattern will result in a different set of rivers, so you might even want to try both.

SCIENCE CONCEPT

When water flows down a mountain, it finds the quickest path to the bottom, even if that path isn't straight. Trees, rocks, and hills cause it to change direction and the speed it travels. When water moves slowly, it tends to dig away at its boundaries (the riverbank), and sometimes will cut out a piece of the bank, which makes the river a little wider at that point. Every time the river changes, the water flow changes and that causes even more variation in the path of the river. So over time, a river can carve out all kinds of interesting paths to the sea. But that's not all. When a new piece of the river is carved out, the current carries rocks and dirt farther downstream. Where this material lands, the river gets shallower. That is why the mouths of rivers, especially where they empty into the ocean, tend to be really wide, open, and flat, with water that moves slowly into the ocean.

MATERIALS

A large mountain of rocks, dirt, sand, mud, and so forth, at least 3 feet high
An open place where the rivers can flow and deposit the mud they accumulate as
    they flow down the mountain
Plenty of water, either through a hose, a sprinkler, or a watering can
Camera

PROCEDURE

1. Make sure the mountain is not the same all over. There should be obstacles all over it that will encourage the water to flow in interesting paths.

2. Predict where the rivers will form.

3. Choose a method of watering:

   Steady rain—Use a sprinkler on top of the mountain, or very near the edge of it to produce rainfall that will be steady throughout the experiment. A helpful assistant could simply hold a hose above the mountain or spray the water onto the top of the mountain. You may need to experiment to find what works best.

   Occasional rain—Use a watering can, a pitcher of water, or a short interval of rain from a hose. If you choose this method, you will need to return every hour or so to add more water. This allows the mountain to absorb some of the water and will result in a different set of rivers.

4. Begin watering the mountain.

5. If you are using a steady rain, take a picture before you begin, and then take a picture every 5 to 10 minutes until the rivers are no longer changing. Your goal is to observe the changes in the mountain over time. It's better to have too many photos than to have too few.

    If you choose the occasional rain method, take a picture before you begin and then during each rainfall. Apply the water for as long as you have chosen and then let the mountain sit until the next session. Repeat applications until the rivers stop changing. This method will likely take quite a bit longer than the other, but might give a more accurate depiction of true rainfall.

6. Keep a record of your method and the photos you took.

7. When you get the photos developed, you should have a record of the progress of the rivers you produced. If you find that the photos don't show enough change, use every other picture.

QUESTIONS FOR THE SCIENTIST

• Did the rivers form in the places you predicted?

• How much material was carried off the mountain to the surrounding area?

• Did you see any smaller rivers merge into larger rivers?

• Was there one river that changed its path more than the rest? If so, what were some of the characteristics of that river that made it change so much?

CONCLUSION

Each time you repeat this experiment, you will get a different result. That's part of the fun of science! Now that you've produced your own rivers, see if you can visit a local river and identify places where it veered over time, where it moves faster or slower than other places, and any obstacles that might affect the flow of water. Also, see if you can trace the source of the river, although it might be many miles away in the mountains.

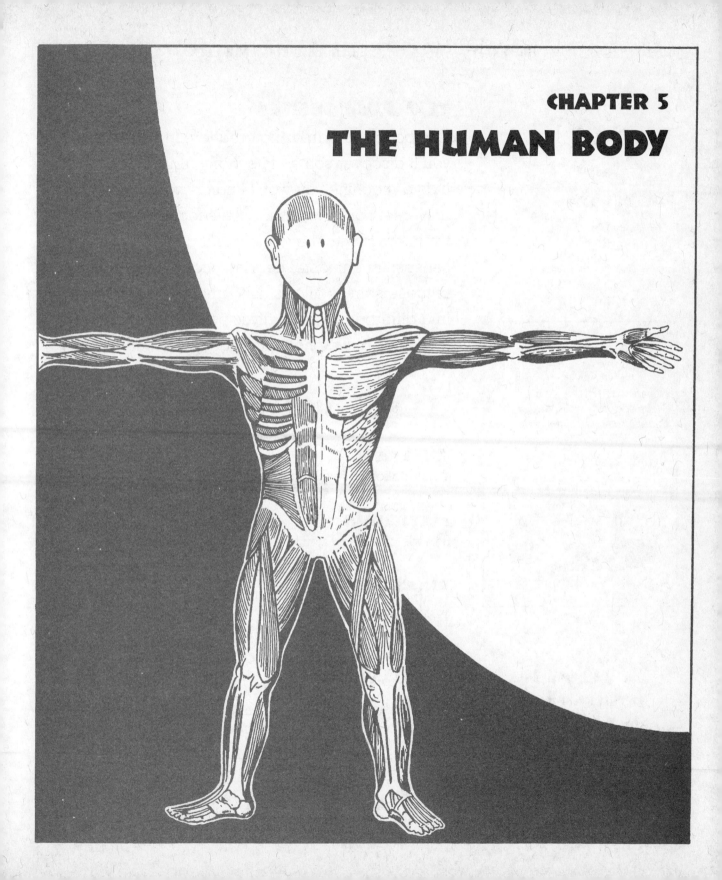

CHAPTER 5
THE HUMAN BODY

Science Online

For more fun activities involving your five senses, check out Neuroscience for Kids. Visit *http://faculty.washington.edu/ chudler/chsense.html*

What did the clever scientist invent that was full of holes but could still hold water?

A sponge!

THE FIVE SENSES

Our body is an amazing creation. In this chapter, you'll discover some of its many abilities that qualify it as a machine you won't find anywhere else in the universe. For now, though, let's focus on the ways we interact with the world around us. We have five senses: touch, taste, hearing, sight, and smell. Each of these senses allows us to understand the world in a different way and gives us a unique perspective on what we encounter each day.

TRY THIS HOT AND COLD

QUESTION
What makes us feel hot and cold?

MATERIALS
3 bowls of water: 1 warm, 1 cold, and 1 at room temperature.

PROCEDURE

1. Arrange the bowls of water in front of you from left to right as follows: warm, room temperature, cold.

2. Place your left hand in the bowl of warm water and your right hand in the bowl of cold water for 30 seconds.

3. Remove your hands from the water and place both into the middle bowl (room temperature).

WHAT'S HAPPENING

Hot and cold are just a way of comparing what we are used to with what we are feeling. Your left hand was used to warm water, so when you placed it into the bowl with water at room temperature, it felt quite cold. On the other side, your right hand was used to cold water, so when you placed it into room-temperature water, it felt warm. Both hands were in the same water, but since they were used to different temperatures, one felt cold and the other felt warm.

FOLLOW-UP

Next time you take a bath or a shower, think about how the bathroom air feels when you get out. Ask someone who is dry to tell you how the air feels and see if you can explain why you perceive the air differently. Another place to try this is at a swimming pool. Try to explain how warm or cold the air and water feel when you are dry and when you are wet. Heat flows naturally from warm objects to cool objects and makes us feel warm or cold as a result.

Did you hear about the scientist who invented a gas that could burn through anything ?

Wow, that's terrific!

No, it's terrible—now he's trying to invent something to keep it in!

TRY THIS TASTELESS MEDICINE

QUESTION

Why can't I taste medicine when I plug my nose?

MATERIALS

Blindfold
Nose plug or your hand
Equal-sized pieces of apple, potato, onion, and jicama
Assistant

PROCEDURE

1. Place the blindfold over your eyes and plug your nose.

2. Have your assistant place one item into your mouth at a time, and try to guess what it is based only on how it tastes.

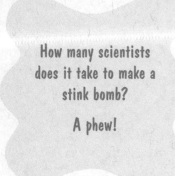

How many scientists does it take to make a stink bomb?

A phew!

Cool Quotes

Smell is a potent wizard that transports us across thousands of miles and all the years we have lived.

—Helen Keller

WHAT'S HAPPENING

Your sense of smell is a major factor in how food items taste. When your nose is plugged, you lose your normal ability to taste. Aside from their textures, you probably couldn't detect the difference between the items you tasted. When you unplug your nose, all the flavors should come back, although the strongest ones might overwhelm the others.

FOLLOW-UP

Have you ever had a really bad cold? If so, you might remember that your food tasted pretty bland. When your nose is stuffed up, you again lose the sense of taste that you are accustomed to. As soon as your cold cleared up, you were able to taste things again!

What's Going On?

Can you figure out these small picture clues? When you think of a word to go with each picture, fit it in the grid going up and down. Then you will need to add some extra letters to the shaded row. When you're finished, you will have the name of a group of important body functions. We gave you the *E*s to help you complete this experiment!

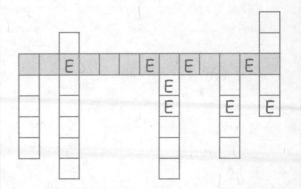

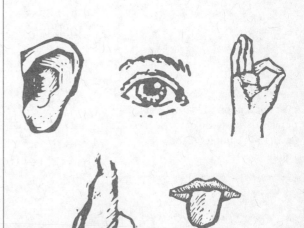

KIDS' LAB LESSONS

QUESTION   How can I taste different flavors?

EXPERIMENT OVERVIEW   In this experiment you will place different food items on different locations of your tongue to determine which **taste buds** can sense which flavors. You'll test sweet, sour, bitter, and salty.

SCIENCE CONCEPT   Our tongue has thousands of tiny taste buds on it. Each one reacts to a certain kind of taste. Taste buds that respond to the same taste are grouped together in certain locations on your tongue. Therefore, you will always taste salty foods in certain places, sweet foods in other places, and sour and bitter foods in still other places, no matter what food you are eating.

WORDS to KNOW

taste buds: little organs all over our tongues that interpret or pick up the sense of what flavors are in our food and liquids.

MATERIALS
Cotton swabs
Small bowls containing the following:
  Lemon juice
  Water
  Sugar
  Table salt
  Instant coffee
A diagram of the tongue, shown
  on page 103
Marking pen

Fun Facts
A typical human has around 116 taste buds per square centimeter at the tip of the tongue, compared to an average of 25 taste buds per square centimeter near the back of the tongue.

PROCEDURE

1. Dip a cotton swab in the lemon juice and spread it around your mouth.
2. Mark on the diagram where on your tongue you sensed this sour taste.
3. Dip a second cotton swab in water and then into the sugar. Spread enough around in your mouth so that you can tell where your tongue senses this sweet taste.
4. Repeat this same procedure with the salt and the instant coffee (a bitter taste).
5. Record on the picture the locations where you sensed each taste.
6. Check your picture to make sure that you have covered each part of the tongue. If you missed one, repeat the experiment to find the taste sensed by that part of the tongue.

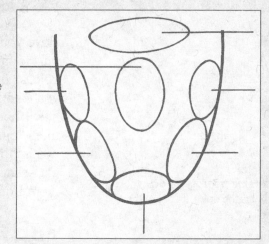

QUESTIONS FOR THE SCIENTIST

• Which parts of the tongue responded to sour?_____

• Which parts of the tongue responded to sweet?_____

• Which parts of the tongue responded to salty?_____

• Which parts of the tongue responded to bitter? _____

• Does your diagram of the tongue explain the location of sores after eating too much sugar? _____

_____

FOLLOW-UP

Try other foods that you know to be in one of these four categories. When you eat them, try to see if you can taste them on the part of your tongue that you marked in this experiment. Try plugging your nose and testing for these four tastes. Does your nose affect your ability to recognize tastes?[1]

TRY THIS CYAN, BLACK, AND YELLOW

Have you ever looked at a picture that had really bright colors only to find that when you looked away, you saw even more colors, though different from the ones in the picture? If so, you've experienced another side of afterimages. You learned a little about these earlier in the book (see page 64), but there's more to the story. Your eyes have the ability not only to "see" two images at a time, as you discovered in the "Bird Cage" experiment, but they can also block certain colors and keep them from being seen.

WORDS to KNOW

complementary color: a color that is the opposite of another color.

QUESTION

What colors can you see in an afterimage?

MATERIALS

Several sheets of paper
Marking pens, including blue, red, green, black, yellow, and cyan (like turquoise or teal)
Color picture of the American flag

PROCEDURE

1. On your first three sheets of paper, draw large circles. On sheet one filling the circle in red. On sheet two make it blue, and on sheet three make it green.

2. In order, focus your eyes on each of the circles (one at a time) for about 30 seconds.

3. After focusing on each of the circles, either look at a blank sheet of white paper or simply close your eyes. Describe the colors you see.

4. Next, focus your eyes on the picture of the American flag, again for about 30 seconds.

5. Look away and describe the new colors of the flag you see as an afterimage.

6. Try to draw an afterimage American flag. Make the stripes black and cyan, while the stars should also be black, but set on a yellow background. Use the picture of the actual flag as a guide.

7. When you are done, focus intently on your flag, then look away. Do you see the true colors of the flag?

WHAT'S HAPPENING

Your eyes use cones to detect colors. When you focus your eyes on a certain color, like green, your cones work extra hard to help you see that color. Then, when you look away, the cones for that color relax and temporarily don't work as well. Therefore you see everything but the original color. The term for what you see is **complementary color.** Can you tell which colors you see as afterimages of red, green, and blue?[2]

When you viewed the American flag, your cones focused on red, white, and blue. When you relaxed your eyes by looking away, the afterimage you saw was of the complementary colors of red, white, and blue. Those colors are cyan, black, and yellow.

FOLLOW-UP

Figure out which eye is your dominant one. Try the following test:

• Hold up a tube to your eye—which eye do you close and which do you use to sight through the tube? _____

I Can't Believe My Eyes!

Do your eyes always see things in just one way? No! Optical illusions are a kind of puzzle designed to fool your eyes (and your brain). See if you can tell the difference between illusion and reality in the following puzzles.

Do you see a 13 or a B in the center of the figures above?

What do you see where the white lines cross?

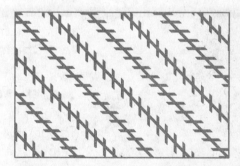

Are the long black lines parallel (even) with each other, or are they crooked?

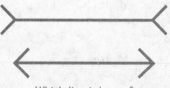

Which line is longer?

KIDS' LAB LESSONS

QUESTION   How does my eye work?

EXPERIMENT OVERVIEW   In this experiment you'll build a model that shows you what kinds of **images** your eyes form. You can determine the size of the image and will see how to extend this concept to building a **pinhole camera**.

SCIENCE CONCEPT   Your eye is a complex device designed to gather light, focus it onto your retina, and send signals to your brain about what you are seeing. The **lens** of your eye takes light rays from all around you and focuses them to a single spot on the back of your eye. There, the rods and cones turn that image into something your brain can understand. As complex as your eye is, you can build a model of your eye that produces an image that is quite similar to what your eye produces.

WORDS to KNOW

image: what we see when we look at something. The image is formed in our head and transferred to our brain.

pinhole camera: a device which allows you to look at an object indirectly.

lens: an optical device that bends light rays and makes it possible for us to see.

MATERIALS
Safety pin
Paper cup
Rubber band
Wax paper
Bare light bulb, turned on

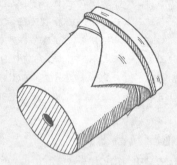

PROCEDURE
1. Poke a small hole with the pin in the bottom of the cup. If you want to make it bigger later on, you can. For now, keep it pretty small.

2. Use the rubber band to secure a square of wax paper across the top of the cup. This will be your screen.
3. Point the bottom of the cup at the light bulb from a distance of 2 to 3 feet.
4. Slowly move toward the light while keeping a close eye on the wax paper.
5. When you get close enough, you will see an image of the light bulb on the wax paper, but it will be upside down.

Fun Facts

Worker bees have 5,500 lenses in each eye.

The first pinhole cameras were actually rooms that were very dark except for a small hole in one wall that let light in. In fact, the Italian word for room is "camera"!

QUESTIONS FOR THE SCIENTIST

• How close did you get to the light before you could see the light bulb's image on the wax paper? _____
• How does this distance change if you make the hole in the bottom of the cup slightly bigger? _____

• Why is the image upside down? _____

• How is this similar to the way a camera works? _____

FOLLOW-UP

Now that you have built this model of your eye, you are ready to build a pinhole camera, which operates on many of the same principles.

You will need a ruler, an empty can of Pringles potato chips, a knife (with help from an adult), a thumbtack, tape, and aluminum foil.

1. Measure 2 to 3 inches from the bottom of the can and have an adult cut the tube into two smaller tubes.
2. Use the thumbtack to poke a small hole in the bottom of the smaller tube and place the plastic lid of the original can on top.
3. Place the larger tube on top of the smaller tube so that the lid lies between them. Tape these together to re-form the original tube.
4. Wrap aluminum foil around the whole tube. This needs to keep as much light out as possible so make sure you cover the entire can.
5. Hold the open end close to your eye and look into the tube. You should see inverted images projected on the screen (the plastic lid).

Fun Facts

Swimmer Amy van Dyken won four gold medals at the 1996 Olympic Games in Atlanta despite having only 65 percent of the lung capacity of an average person due to asthma.

Why did the scientist take his nose apart?

He wanted to see what made it run!

HUMAN MACHINE

Human beings have produced some remarkable **machines** in the past hundred years or so. The airplane, the automobile, and the computer are just a few examples of machines invented by ordinary people that have forever changed our lives. But if you want to see a machine that is more complex, more beautiful, and more unique than any of these, look in the mirror. Our bodies are capable of things that no machine will ever be able to accomplish, no matter how powerful computers get. As we wrap this book up, let's take a look at some of the wonderful things human bodies can do.

TRY THIS DEEP BREATH

QUESTION
How much air can my **lungs** hold?

MATERIALS
Large, empty 1-gallon glass jar
32-ounce (quart) glass jar
Water
Large flat container, for example, an aquarium
Permanent marker
3 flat stones or other flat items
Sink or location that can get wet
18 to 24 inches of rubber tubing
1 sheet of paper
1 writing utensil

PROCEDURE

1. Fill the large jar by repeatedly filling the 32-ounce jar with water and emptying it into the large jar.

2. After each quart of water is added, make a mark on the jar indicating the height of one quart.

3. Fill the aquarium about three-quarters full of water and place the stones in a circle on the bottom.

4. Place the aquarium in the sink. Carefully turn the large jar over and place it on the stones on the bottom of the aquarium. Don't worry if some water spills out.

5. Make a note of the initial water level in the jar. This will be your starting point.

6. Place one end of the rubber tubing into the aquarium and under the mouth of the jar. Let the other end hang over the side of the aquarium.

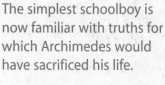

Cool Quotes

The simplest schoolboy is now familiar with truths for which Archimedes would have sacrificed his life.

—Ernest Renan, French philosopher and theologian

7. Take a deep breath and blow into the free end of the rubber tubing.

8. Measure the resulting mark of the water in the jar.

9. Subtract the original mark to find your lung capacity in quarts.

WHAT'S HAPPENING

When you blow air out of your lungs and into the jar, it replaces some of the water. The water level will rise in the aquarium. You can measure how much air was added to the jar to see how much air your lungs held. Try this experiment again and see if you can improve your results.

The silly scientist discovered something that has a bottom at the top—what is it?

Your legs!

Fun Facts

The typical human reaction time in an experiment like the one you performed is around 0.20 seconds.

Science Online

Visit a human body online at www.pa.k12.ri.us/Curric/Science/Human1.htm

TRY THIS ACTION-REACTION

Every time someone gets into a car to drive, they must make decisions that will keep them safe. Some of them can be made slowly, for example, whether or not to roll the window down, while others must be made very quickly, such as swerving to avoid a collision with another car.

QUESTION

What is my reaction time?

MATERIALS

Dollar bill or note card
Friend
Ruler

PROCEDURE

1. Hold the dollar bill vertically lengthwise with one hand while placing your other hand's thumb and forefinger near the bottom of it.

2. Drop the bill and catch it with your other hand. You should be able to do this easily.

3. Now have your friend do the dropping. You should not know when the bill is to be dropped.

Cool Quotes

Every science begins as philosophy and ends as art.

—Will Durant

WHAT'S HAPPENING

When you dropped the bill, your brain was able to send a signal to your other hand telling it to start catching it. When your friend dropped the bill, you didn't have that head start, so you got a more accurate reading for your reaction time. The lower on the bill you were able to catch it, the faster your reaction time. If you weren't able to catch it at all, you aren't alone. Try dropping a ruler instead.[3]

FOLLOW-UP

This reaction time test is one of many you could do. See if you can come up with your own test.

_____

_____

_____

_____

_____

I See!

If you are conducting experiments you must use your powers of observation—that means you must look very carefully at your information so as not to miss an important detail! Practice your powers by finding the 10 differences between these two pictures.

KIDS' LAB LESSONS

QUESTION   What is my **pulse**?

EXPERIMENT OVERVIEW   In this experiment you'll be measuring your pulse (heart rate) after several different activities. You'll also learn how to use different time intervals to measure your heart rate and where the best places are to find your heartbeat.

SCIENCE CONCEPT   Each time your heart beats it delivers oxygen-rich blood to your body, which allows it to function properly. When you are resting, your heart rate slows down, as your body doesn't need as much blood as it does when you exercise. People who are in good physical condition are able to engage in strenuous activities while keeping their heart rate low. On your body, the strongest beats can usually be felt over your heart, in your neck just below your jaw, on the inside of your wrists, and on your thumbs.

WORDS to KNOW

pulse/heart rate: how many times per minute your heart beats.

MATERIALS   Stopwatch

PROCEDURE
1. Sit quietly for a few minutes before beginning this test.
2. When you are ready, place your first two fingers either on your neck or on the inside of your wrist and locate your pulse.
3. Once you find your pulse, start the watch and for 60 seconds, count the number of beats you feel. That is your pulse.

4. Try the experiment again, but this time count for only 30 seconds. When you are done, multiply your count by two. Compare your pulses.

5. Repeat by counting for 15 seconds and multiplying your count by four, then counting for 10 seconds and multiplying by six.

6. Once you have determined your resting pulse, go somewhere that you can exercise vigorously for at least one minute. Exercise of this sort might include a fast jog, running stairs, skipping rope, or doing pushups. When you are done, you should be breathing hard. CAUTION: Do not exert yourself beyond what you are comfortable with. Pick an activity you can do safely.

7. Choose the length of the test you wish to perform and find your pulse again.

8. Compare your resting pulse with your pulse after exercise.

QUESTIONS FOR THE SCIENTIST

• What was your resting pulse? _____
• Which result(s) did you use to come up with this number? _____
• What was your pulse after exercise? _____
• What are the advantages to timing for a full minute to find your pulse? _____
• What are the advantages to timing over a shorter period of time (like 10 seconds), especially when you have just finished exercising? _____
• The American Heart Association has determined that the maximum heart rate should be 220 minus a person's age. Was your highest rate below that number?

_____

FOLLOW-UP

Regular exercise can reduce both your resting heart rate and your heart rate after exercise. For a long-term study of your own heart rate, try exercising for 15 to 20 minutes daily for one month. Once a week, recheck your heart rates before and after exercise to see if they go down. If you plan on drastically changing your exercise patterns, check with your parents or your doctor to make sure the change is appropriate for you.

balance: your ability to stay standing without falling over.

Fun Facts

One of the most natural and effective cures for motion sickness is ginger. Some people eat gingersnap cookies, while others drink ginger ale.

What kind of scientist studies shopping?

A buy-ologist!

TRY THIS BLIND BALANCE

One of the most fun things to do as a kid is to spin around really fast and get dizzy. Our sense of **balance** comes from our ears and the liquid inside them that sometimes gets sloshed around. When it calms down, the dizziness generally goes away. Balance is a difficult condition to understand. So is the question of why some people get dizzy riding in the back seat of a car or on a boat while others can ride the wildest roller coasters or perform as gymnasts or figure skaters and never get the slightest bit dizzy.

QUESTION

Is it harder to balance with your eyes closed?

MATERIALS

None

PROCEDURE

1. Stand on both feet in the middle of the room.

2. Try to balance for 30 seconds.

3. Close both eyes and try to balance for 30 seconds. Compare the difficulty of the two tasks.

4. Stand on one leg and balance for 15 seconds. Do not touch anything for support.

5. Close your eyes, stand on one leg, and try to balance for 15 seconds.

WHAT'S HAPPENING

Much of your sense of balance comes from your ability to see your surroundings. When you lose the ability to measure your balance with respect to the room (by closing your eyes) you have a harder time keeping your balance. People who get seasick on a boat have a similar problem. They look out at the land and water and it's all moving. Since there is no fixed point that they can look at, they lose their balance (and sometimes much more).

FOLLOW-UP

Try standing very close to a wall and repeating the experiment with one leg and both legs. This time, lightly touch the wall. Try not to use it for balance, just to remind you that it's there. Does it help you stay balanced?[4]

_____

_____

Boy, Do You Look Familiar!

Do parents and their children look exactly alike? No, but often people can pick family members out of a group. Study the following faces and see if you can do it, too. Draw a line matching each pair of relatives.

KIDS' LAB LESSONS

WORDS to KNOW

center of gravity: your body's balance point.

QUESTION Where is my **center of gravity**?

EXPERIMENT OVERVIEW In this experiment you'll perform several physical tasks along with other people to determine the differences between the center of gravity of a man and a woman, as well as the differences between kids and adults.

SCIENCE CONCEPT Every object has a center of gravity. It is the part of the object that must be supported to keep from falling over. Adult men and women have different centers of gravity, as you will see. Kids, due to the fact that they have not yet physically developed like adults have, don't always show those same differences.

MATERIALS Adults and kids of both sexes   Coffee cup
Wall   Stool

PROCEDURE Have each participant try these tasks. See who can complete them.

Test 1
1. Stand next to a wall so that one side of your body, including your foot, is touching the wall.
2. Try to lift your other foot off the ground and stay standing.

Test 2
1. Place the coffee cup 8 to 10 inches in front of your feet while standing in the middle of a room.
2. Bend over and pick up the cup.
3. Now move so that you are standing with your back and feet to a wall.

4. Place the cup 8 to 10 inches in front of you and try to bend over and pick it up.
5. Try to describe why this second task is so difficult. Repeat the original test in the middle of the room if you wish.

Test 3
1. Kneel on the floor and place the coffee cup the length of your forearm in front of your knees.
2. Place your hands behind your back and try to knock the cup over with your nose.

Test 4
1. Stand with your feet together, about 2 feet in front of a wall.
2. Have someone place a stool between your feet and the wall.
3. Lean toward the wall until your forehead is touching it. Keep your back straight while you do this.
4. Pick up the stool and hold it to your chest.
5. From this position, try to straighten your back and stand up.

- Is there a difference in performance between men and women, or between adults and kids, for the first two tests?
- Is there a difference in performance between men and women, or between adults and kids, for the last two tests?
- Thinking about the idea of center of gravity, why do you suppose women have an easier time with the last two tests than men do?
- Kids tend to do better on these final tasks than adult men do. Can you think of a reason why this might be?

QUESTIONS FOR THE SCIENTIST
- In Test 1, why do you fall immediately when you lift your outside leg?
- Try this same test in the middle of the room. Why don't you fall?
- Why are you able to pick up the cup while standing in the middle of the room, but you can't reach it with your back against the wall?

FOLLOW-UP
Think up other interesting tests you can perform to test for center of gravity.[5] Also, think of jobs or sports that require good balance and a knowledge of center of gravity. Do you engage in an activity that requires you to keep your balance? If so, think about where your center of gravity is during that activity.

SCIENCE FAIR PROJECT: HUMAN BODY

GENETICS

Perhaps people have told you that you "look just like your mother" or that you "have your father's eyes." If you have siblings, you may see no resemblance, while others say, "I can tell you are related." What is it about our looks that says so much about who we are and where we came from? The answer lies in our genes—the blueprint for how we are made. Each of us inherits our genes from our biological parents. But some traits or characteristics are more common, or dominant, in our families, while others are recessive, or less likely to occur. We can't easily look inside our genetic code to see what traits we inherited from which parent, but we can use a survey and probability to predict the patterns.

QUESTION

Why are my eyes green?

EXPERIMENT OVERVIEW

In this experiment you and your parents will complete a survey that asks about certain inherited traits, or traits that you have no control over. Then you'll pick two of them to complete a probability study using a tool called a Punnett square.

SCIENCE CONCEPT

Traits like hair or eye color, attached ear lobes, hitchhiker's thumb, and the ability to roll your tongue are called dominant or recessive. Each of us has two genes for each trait in us—one we inherited from our mother and one from our father. As you might expect, a person who has two dominant genes or two recessive genes will have that trait. However, a person with one of each will display the trait of the dominant gene even though they possess the recessive gene as well. Here's an example.

Suppose you own two black rabbits and they produce a baby rabbit. In rabbits, black fur is a dominant gene (shown as a capital letter) and brown is a recessive gene (shown as a lowercase letter). Let's suppose in this case that your two rabbits each have a black and a brown fur gene. Can you explain why they both have black fur? When they have a baby, the baby will inherit one of the many combinations of fur genes from its parents—either two blacks, a brown and a black, or two browns. In the first two cases, the baby will also have black fur. There is actually a 75 percent chance that this will happen. But there is a 25 percent chance that the baby will inherit both parents' brown fur genes and will be born with brown fur. That is, two black rabbits can produce a brown rabbit.

The Punnett square below shows how this could happen.

FATHER

	Black	brown
Black	BB (Black)	Bb (Black)
brown	bB (Black)	bb (brown)

MOTHER

So if both of your parents have brown eyes but yours are green, that is a perfectly reasonable possibility.

MATERIALS

Survey (at the end of the chapter)
You and your biological parents. If this isn't possible, find someone who has access to his or her biological parents and ask him to help you.
Punnett square
2 coins

PROCEDURE

1. Complete the survey; then ask each of your parents to complete it as well. If you can think of other traits to include, add them.

2. Talk with your parents about the results. Discuss how many of the traits of each parent you have.

3. Pick two of the traits for the second part of the experiment. One should be a trait that both parents have in common but you do not have, if possible. Otherwise, just pick a trait that you all have in common. The second should be a trait that your parents differ on.

4. For each trait you select, build a Punnett square that could produce your family's results. A sample is shown below. Mother has green eyes, father has brown eyes, child has green eyes. In this case, the brown gene is dominant over the green gene. This could occur in either of the combinations on the right.

FATHER

	Brown	green
green	Bq (Brown)	qq (green)
green	gB (Brown)	gg (green)

MOTHER

5. Count the number of smaller squares that could produce your results. For the example above, there are two.

6. Divide this number by four, the total number of squares, to determine the probability, or chance, of this result occurring. For this example, the probability is 50 percent.

7. On a piece of paper, decide which gene will be represented by heads and which will be tails for each coin you will be flipping. It might be easier to use different coins to represent each parent.

8. Toss both coins 20 times for each trait. Count the number of times you get a result that matches your own results (in our example, the result we're looking for is that the child has green eyes) and divide that number by 20. This is your experimental probability.

9. Compare your experimental probability with your theoretical probability and present your findings.

QUESTIONS FOR THE SCIENTIST

• Are there any traits that your parents share but that you do not possess? What are they?

• Are there traits that all three of you share?

• Do you think these traits are carried by dominant or recessive genes?

- How close were your experimental results to the values you calculated from the Punnett square?

- What does it mean if your results don't match your predictions?

- Does the Punnett square mean that if a mother and father have four children each child will fit into one of the squares? Why or why not?

CONCLUSION

Genetics is one of the most fascinating and scary topics in biological research today. From cloning to disease prevention, doctors are searching for ways to improve our lives by understanding what it is we are made of. So far, there is no guaranteed way to predict the traits of one's children, and that's probably a good thing. However, an understanding of your past helps you prepare for your future and that's one of the many reasons why children who are adopted try to find their birth parents. No matter who we are, it's reassuring to know that we didn't happen by chance, and that there is a plan, however complex it may be, for our being who we are.

SURVEY

1. Can you roll your tongue? Stick out your tongue. Try to curl it into a u. Write "yes" or "no."
You_____
Mother_____
Father_____

2. Are you right or left thumbed? Put your hands together, interlocking your fingers. Which thumb is on top? Write "right" or "left."
You_____
Mother_____
Father_____

3. Do you have dimples? Smile at a friend. Do they see any dimples? Write "yes" or "no."
You_____

Mother_____
Father_____

4. Are your earlobes attached or unattached? Write "attached" or "unattached."
You_____
Mother_____
Father_____

5. Do you have "hitchhiker's thumb" (curved thumb when you stick it straight out)? Write "yes" or "no."
You_____
Mother_____
Father_____

FINAL THOUGHTS

After reading this book, you may find yourself wishing there were more activities to try. Perhaps the questions you were able to address by doing the experiments here only brought up more questions for which you don't have answers. If either is the case for you, then congratulations! You are a scientist!

You see, scientists are never satisfied that they know all there is to know. Each answer brings more questions. They are filled with an insatiable desire to know more about their world. When they can't find the answers in a book, they figure out ways to predict what the answers should be and then test those predictions, according to the Scientific Method. But

would you like to know a secret? Scientists aren't the only people who use this method. Lawyers, doctors, bankers, teachers, stockbrokers, and real estate agents do, too. In fact, you'd be hard-pressed to find anyone who doesn't use the principles of the Scientific Method in his or her daily life.

So welcome to the world of science! Ask questions; dig deep to find answers; don't accept "I don't know" for an answer; and, most of all, have fun (and be safe!) doing it. For it is in the search for answers that the true wonder and beauty of this world will be revealed to you.

NOTES

Chapter 1

1. *Water Colors (page 3)*—You should usually water the ground around your plants, not just the leaves. While some water is absorbed through leaves, the plant will get its water more easily by the process you saw in the experiment—through its roots in the ground.

2. *Falling Leaves (page 5)*—The leaves change color when the days begin to get shorter. With less light, the trees are not able to produce as much chlorophyll, and this begins the process of falling leaves.

3. *Blue Blockers (page 16)*—The sunglasses do in fact block nearly all of the blue light that hits them. As a result, you shouldn't see much of the color blue when you look around. What you will see, however, is a lot of color that isn't blue. The term for this is *complement*, and the complement of blue is yellow. Do you see yellow? Actually, yellow light is made up of two other colors: red and green. So you should notice rich greens and reds as well.

4. *Walking on Eggshells (page 19)*—Both the bed-of-nails trick and snowshoes use the same principle as the egg experiment. While a single nail would pierce a person's skin, using hundreds of nails spreads the weight of the person's body evenly over the whole bed and no single nail has to hold more weight than it can handle. The performer isn't hurt. NOTE: Magicians are professionals who practice under very safe conditions. Never try a "trick" like that at your own home!

If you tried to walk in very deep snow in your regular shoes, you would probably fall right through. A snowshoe spreads your weight evenly over its whole shape (kind of like a tennis racket). By distributing your weight, no part of the snow has to hold more weight than it can, and you stay on top of the snow. See if you can find more examples of this weight-spreading phenomenon in nature!

Chapter 2

1. *Boiling Ice (page 25)*—When the ice melts into liquid water, it is still very cold. In fact, it's 0°C (32°F), just like the ice was. Water can boil only when it is all at 100°C (212°F), so before it can start boiling again, all the melted ice must be warmed up to 100°C. Once all the water in the pot is at that temperature, it will begin boiling once more.

2. *Cleaning Pennies (page 41)*—The other coins listed are not coated with copper. The cleaning reaction works only with a weak acid (like the vinegar/salt solution) and copper. You won't get the same results with the other coins.

Chapter 3

1. *Seesaw (page 49)*—Two pennies 6 inches away will balance, as would one penny located 12 inches away. Unfortunately, on this ruler, the farthest you can get away from the fulcrum is 6 inches. Another combination that would work would be eight pennies located 1½ inches from the fulcrum (because 8 × 1½ = 12).

2. *Teeter-Totter (page 49)*—The heavier person needs to sit closer to the middle (the fulcrum) so his or her weight doesn't count as much. With your parents, the weight difference might be big, especially if you are young. Your parent might have to sit almost at the middle to make the teeter-totter balance, but it can be done.

3. *Cushioning the Blow (page 51)*—Some examples: boxers wear padded gloves; bicycles have padded seats; tennis shoes have padded soles; air bags in cars soften the impact in an accident; and catchers in baseball use a soft, oversized mitt to catch pitches.

4. *Corners (page 55)*—Helium is lighter than air, so unlike most objects, it doesn't fall to the ground. Instead, it rises upward, toward the sky. When the car turns, everything in the car wants to keep moving in a straight line except the balloon. It wants to follow the turn. For more fun, watch what a balloon does when you speed up and slow down in a car. You'll soon see why balloons in a car can be a safety hazard.

5. *Magnetic Electricity (page 61)*—The electromagnet formed by the electricity works only when the battery is attached. When you disconnect it, the compass returns to normal. However, when you place the wire under the compass, the magnet formed by the electricity is flipped so it points in the opposite direction. Thus, the compass also points in the opposite direction.

6. *Electromagnet (page 63)*—One of the most common places you'll find electromagnets of this kind is a wrecking yard. There they use a crane with an electromagnet turned on to lift large vehicles into the air, and when they are ready to drop them into their new location, they simply turn the magnet off and the vehicle drops.

Chapter 4

1. *Wind Speed (page 77)*—First, you need to measure the radius of your anemometer (the distance from one of the cups to the center of your device) in inches. Then you multiply that number by 6.28 to find the circumference, or the distance a cup will travel in one complete circle. Now, count the number of circles, or revolutions, the marked cup makes in one minute. Multiply this number times your circumference and you'll have a speed in inches per minute. To convert this speed to miles per hour, simply divide this final result by 1,056 and you'll have your speed in miles per hour.

Example:

Your radius is approximately 8 inches. This makes a circumference of 8 × 6.28 = 50.24 inches. If you count 40 revolutions in one minute, then the cup travels a total of 40 × 50.24 inches = 2,010 inches in one minute. Divide this result by 1,056 and you get a speed of 1.9 miles per hour.

2. *Land Warmer (page 81)*—Only the top layer of sand gets warm on a typical beach. The sun cannot reach the lower levels of sand, so it isn't able to heat those levels. For the same reason, the top layer of water in a pool or even a small lake is often warmer than deeper water.

3. *Icicles (page 83)*—Epsom salts is often used to help heal bruises and sprains. It is also used in the production of high fructose corn syrup, something you'll find in most soft drinks. One of its most popular uses is in bathtubs for people who want to soak and relax. If you have problems with raccoons, you can sprinkle it around your garbage cans and it will drive the raccoons off without harming them. As an added benefit, it is great food for your plants, too!

4. *Space of Air (page 85)*—In the summer, balls can become very bouncy when left in the sun, but in the winter they become a little flat if left in the cold. Also, if you keep juice in your refrigerator in a pitcher with a cap or tight lid, take it out and let it sit on the counter for a few minutes with the lid still closed. When you finally open the lid, you'll hear the air escape. For another fun experiment, blow up a small balloon and place it in the freezer. You'll be able to see the effects of air compressing as it cools.

5. *Constellations (page 90)*—Look toward the north for what appears to be a large cup with a handle. This is called the Big Dipper, but it is actually part of a larger constellation called Ursa Major—the Great Bear. Look on a star chart to see the shape of the bear. Using the two stars at the far right of the dipper, trace a straight line upward until you encounter another star. It isn't the brightest star in the sky, but it's an important one. It's the North Star (Polaris) and it indicates the direction of due north.

The North Star is actually part of a constellation called the Little Dipper, or Ursa Minor. Some people say that the Little Dipper pours its contents into the Big Dipper.

Other interesting constellations to find include Orion, the hunter (recognizable by his "belt," which is made up of three stars in a row), which is visible throughout the winter months; Cassiopeia, the queen (a *W*-shaped collection of five stars found in the northern skies); Gemini, the twins (winter); Pegasus, the winged horse (autumn); and Leo, the lion (spring). See how many you can find on your own!

Chapter 5

1. *Taste Buds (page 103)*—As you saw earlier, your sense of smell has a major impact on your ability to taste. When your nose is plugged, your taste buds aren't able to send the proper signals to your brain to tell it what kind of flavor they are tasting.

2. *Cyan, Black, and Yellow (page 105)*—The complement of red is cyan, for green it's magenta, and for blue it's yellow. The complement of white (all colors) is black (no colors). That is why a flag of yellow, black, and cyan should produce an afterimage of a flag that is red, white, and blue.

3. *Reaction Time (page 111)*—

If the ruler fell . . .	your reaction time is . . .
4 inches	0.14 seconds
8 inches	0.20 seconds
12 inches	0.25 seconds

4. *Balance (page 115)*—Just having the wall close by serves as a reminder that something is fixed and not moving. You should find it easier to stay standing, especially on one leg, when you lightly touch the wall.

5. *Center of Gravity (page 117)*—Take a yardstick and place your two forefingers under it to support it. It doesn't matter where you put them. Now, slowly move your fingers toward one another, keeping the yardstick balanced. They will meet at the location of the yardstick's center of gravity (usually the middle). You can hang something on one end to change the center of gravity and try it again—you will always find it using this method.

PUZZLE ANSWERS

page x • Quote Fall

T O		T T		O		
Q	H F	S S	M	P	P R	N A N T
T U	E I	I	O	N S	T G	T T

T H E		I M P O R T A N T
T H I N G		I S		N O T
T O		S T O P
Q U E S T I O N I N G

page 12 • Scientific Transformation

1. BANANA
2. BANNAA — *move second N close to first N*
3. BALLAA — *change N to L*
4. BALLOO — *change A to O*
5. BALLOON — *add N*

page 8 • Totally Tubular

END

START

page 17 • Eye Spy

Goose · Owl
Snake · Mouse
Bunny · Snail
Giraffe · Spider
Moth · Hummingbird

PUZZLE ANSWERS

page 31 • Egg-sactly!

Smart person:
EGG <u>HEAD</u>

Money you have saved:
<u>NEST</u> EGG

Colorful treat hunted for in the spring:
<u>EASTER</u> EGG

Words of caution:
DON'T <u>PUT</u> ALL <u>YOUR</u> EGGS IN <u>ONE</u> <u>BASKET</u>.

Word List
EASTER   BASKET
YOUR   NEST
PUT   ONE
HEAD

page 41 • Acid Bath

EMILY
JOHN
NICK
KAITLIN

page 36 • Amazing Bubbles

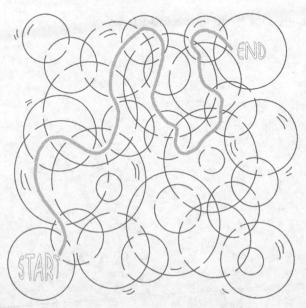

page 55 • Around the Bend

PUZZLE ANSWERS

page 65 • Catchy Categories

Properties of Motion

Properties of Matter

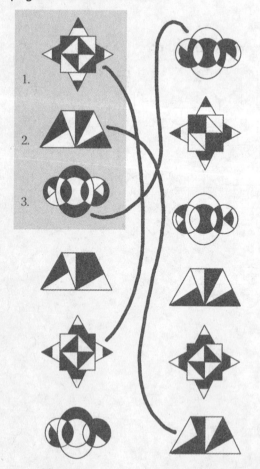

page 67 • Black and White

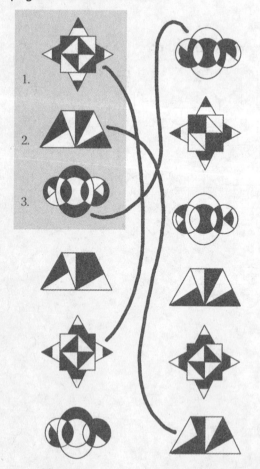

1.
2.
3.

page 75 • Wind Speed

Here are some possible answers:

Three-Letter Words:		Four-Letter Words:		Five-Letter Words:
ant	ram	moan		enter
are	ran	more		manor
arm	rat	name		meant
art	tan	near		meter
ate	tar	neat		tenor
ear	tea	note		
eat	ten	rant		Six-Letter Words:
era	toe	rate		remote
man	ton	rent		rename
mat		roam		moment
men	Four-Letter Words:	rote		meteor
met	amen	tame		
mom	ammo	team		Seven-Letter Word:
net	atom	tear		memento
not	earn	teen		
oar	mane	term		
oat	mare	tone		
one	mate	torn		
ore	mean	tram		
	meat	tree		
	meet			

page 79 • Head in the Clouds

128

PUZZLE ANSWERS

page 81 • **Up or Down?**

A <u>STALACTITE</u>

hangs <u>TIGHT</u> to the ceiling.

A <u>STALAGMITE</u>

grows <u>MIGHTY</u> tall from

the floor.

page 89 • **Sneaky Scientists**

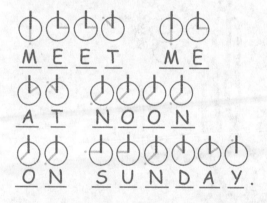

<u>M</u> <u>E</u> <u>E</u> <u>T</u>   <u>M</u> <u>E</u>

<u>A</u> <u>T</u>   <u>N</u> <u>O</u> <u>O</u> <u>N</u>

<u>O</u> <u>N</u>   <u>S</u> <u>U</u> <u>N</u> <u>D</u> <u>A</u> <u>Y</u> .

page 93 • **Giant Science Kriss-Kross**

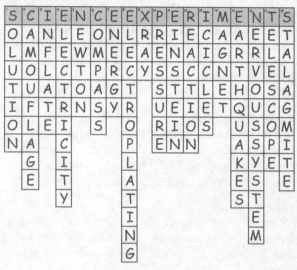

page 101 • **What's Going On?**

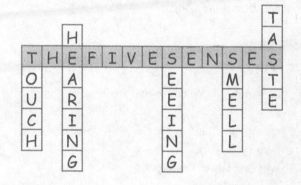

PUZZLE ANSWERS

page 105 • I Can't Believe My Eyes!

13 or B?
You see a number 13 or a capital letter B depending on which way you read, left to right, or top to bottom. Visually, the letters and numbers are so similar that the figure in the middle trick your eyes, and can be read either way.

Crooked Lines or Straight?
The long black lines are parallel to each other. Take a ruler and measure to see that this is true. The short lines that go in different directions fool your eyes into thinking that the long lines are crooked.

Longer or Shorter?
Both lines are the same length. Measure them to see that this is true. The short, slanting lines at the end of the longer lines fools you eyes into thinking the top line is longer.

Where the Lines Cross
You should see flashing grey dots where the white lines cross. What's really interesting is that if you look directly at a gray spot, it disappears!

page 111 • I See!

Differences in the two pictures happen in these places:

1. Flower in girl's hat
2. Lines on girl's socks
3. Leaves on plant in flowerpot
4. Lines on flowerpot
5. Label on watering can
6. Number of checks on calendar
7. Days of week on calendar
8. Spelling of LIGHT on boy's paper
9. Eraser on boy's pencil
10. Hair above boy's ear

page 115 • Boy, Do You Look Familiar!

INDEX